LEAVES FROM THE BOOK OF MY LIFE ...

My Divinely Guided Life

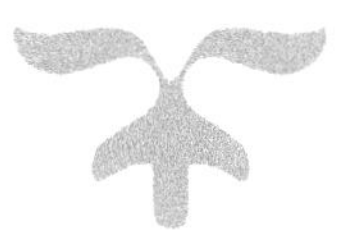

By Dzidra Tagaloa

LEAVES FROM THE BOOK OF MY LIFE...

First published in Australia by Dzidria Tagaloa 2026

A catalogue record for this
book is available from the
National Library of Australia

ISBN: 978-0-646-74107-9 (pbk)

Typesetting and design by Publicious Book Publishing
Published in collaboration with Publicious Book Publishing
www.publicious.com.au

Contents

Introduction

Having lived through the Russian Communist occupation of Latvia, survived capture by the Nazis in Germany, and endured the post-war years in a refugee camp, I look back on my life with a deep sense of awe. When I was accepted as a refugee in New Zealand, I began a new chapter - one that would unfold over fifty years in a land that became my home. Through it all, I can only describe my journey as *divinely guided.*

Now aged 87, with my fifth great-grandchild born, I find myself reflecting on the road I have travelled - and, undoubtedly, the shorter road that remains ahead. In a world still filled with strife and uncertainty, I think often, and with gratitude, of the many moments when my life could have ended suddenly. How many people can say they have escaped death three or even four times? I have. And each time, I felt the presence of something greater - an unseen hand guiding me, protecting me.

Some twenty years ago, I found myself in Australia - this beautiful land we lovingly call "Oz." It is here, in this peaceful chapter of life, that I've had the time to sit quietly and ask myself: *Did it really all happen?* The whole sequence of events that shaped my life, from the terror of war to the joys of motherhood, even the serendipitous moment when I met the man who would become my husband - did it all unfold as it was meant to?

Ours was a mixed-race marriage, nearly taboo in the 1950s. And yet, here we are: three children, five grandchildren, and now six great-grandchildren later - still married after 65 years. He is, without a doubt, my soulmate. So many moments, so many coincidences, so many near-misses and miracles. I can only believe we were brought together by something bigger than ourselves.

In the words of the song:

"I must have done something good."

Chapter 1
The Beginning

But all stories have a beginning.

Mine begins in Latvia, one of the three Baltic States nestled in north-eastern Europe, just across the sea from Sweden. The year was 1939, the beginning of the Second World War - a war that would bring such wretchedness and untold sorrow into the lives of millions. I was one year old.

By this time, Hitler - the Führer of the Nazi Party - had already occupied Paris. In response, Joseph Stalin, the Prime Minister of the Soviet Union, moved quickly. He feared the growing strength of the Third Reich and wanted to act before it became too powerful. The Baltic nations - Latvia, Estonia, and Lithuania - were accused of consorting and conspiring, and an ultimatum was issued: allow Soviet troops to enter peacefully or face bombardment and forcible takeover. Naturally, the governments of the three small nations chose the former - under great pressure and little real choice.

The Russians entered Latvia under the guise of maintaining a "mutual friendship," but the reality was far more sinister. The brutality of the first Soviet occupation (1940–1941) was such that it came to be known as the "Year of Terror."

Latvia was strategically valuable to the Soviet Union. The Gulf of Riga provided access to the open seas - essential for submarines and naval power. Leningrad (now St. Petersburg), much further up the coast, was less practical. Because of this, even today, many Russians consider Latvia their home.

Years later, history would shift again. On 21 August 1991, the Russian Federation, under President Boris Yeltsin, finally recognized Latvian independence. Latvia joined the United Nations on 6 September 1991, and by 31 August 1994, the last of the Russian Army left Latvian territory. The remaining military bases and radar installations were closed by 1998.

Latvian - an Indo-European language related only to Lithuanian - remains the official language. But Russian and German are also widely spoken. Generations of Latvians were forced to learn Russian during Soviet rule, and German has echoed through the region since the days of the Reformation in the 1500s. Add to this a growing use of English, and Latvia today is truly multilingual - even cosmopolitan. I've been told that in Riga, you could name any country in the world and find a café representing it. I believe it.

I was born in 1938, in Riga. Despite the danger, fear, and helplessness that surrounded us, my early memories of childhood are, somehow, still happy ones. My mother worked in the main railway offices; my father also worked on the railways. For a time, I was sent to live with my grandmother, who lived in a small house on the outskirts of Riga.

The street outside ran parallel to the railway line. I still remember peering out as the tanks and the long-barrelled guns rumbled past on the trains - massive, mysterious machines to a child's eyes. I had no idea what they were, only that they were strange and loud and not meant for peace.

My grandfather died near the end of 1938, when I was still just a baby. And yet, I have a vivid image in my mind - crawling toward a low-lying bed in one of the rooms, pointing at a hole in his singlet. Was that a real memory? Or one shaped by the stories my family told me later? I was only eight or nine months old at the time. But somehow, it has stayed with me - that simple moment, in the midst of a world already changing beyond recognition.

Grandad Constantine
(My Mother's dad) & Myself.

Chapter 2
Shadows and Snow

I do remember sitting on a little chair by the window, crawling up carefully to peer outside - waiting to see my grandmother walking down the street, her arms full of parcels from the shops. The street ran alongside the railway line, and sometimes I could see trains pass, the rattle of their wheels echoing off the buildings. It was cold. Snow blanketed everything, and the world looked quiet, almost kind.

Once, I was pulled along on a little sled - bundled up, sliding down that street to the small shopping area. I imagine now it must have been my Grandmother pulling me, for my grandfather had already passed. That simple ride remains one of the purest memories I have of that time - just snow, movement, and care.

Myself and Cousin Zigurds (Latvija)

Another time, I climbed onto a little table by the window, while my grandmother held me steady. I would feed scraps of food to the pigeons on the ledge outside. They would gather there in flurries of feathers, hungry and hopeful. We had little, yet somehow there was always something to share with the birds.

But the memory that stayed with me the longest - one that would later take on a deeper meaning - was far less ordinary.

There was another little girl I used to play with in the street. One day, she invited me to come and meet her grandmother. I followed her inside her home, not knowing I was being taken to witness death for the first time. Her grandmother had passed away, and as was the custom, her body lay in the front room on a low bed, dressed and surrounded by flowers, with candles burning gently at her head.

To my child's eyes, it was breathtaking. I stood in awe. The candles glowed like stars, the flowers gave off a soft fragrance, and the woman lying there looked peaceful, even regal. I just wanted to keep looking. I didn't feel scared - only drawn in by the beauty and stillness of it.

Eventually, the girl's mother noticed me and gently reminded me that my grandmother might be looking for me. I went home, brimming with wonder at what I had seen.

But when I told my grandmother, she was horrified - angry even. She scolded me for going somewhere without permission, but her anger faded quickly as she saw I wasn't upset. I was excited, reverent. I told her everything - about the flowers, the candles, and the beauty. That memory never faded. Years later, it became a quiet strength in me, a preparation for what was to come - a lesson, perhaps, planted by something greater.

Not long after that, I was sent away from my grandmother's home. It seemed I had outstayed my time there. Perhaps my younger brother, Albert, had replaced me. He was two years younger, and my mother, Lidija Rošans, could no longer keep him in the railway office crèche - maybe he had become too boisterous.

That transition marked a change, and with it came one last, painful memory of our family home. I remember being in a crowded room, people laughing and drinking - perhaps it was a christening for Albert and me, though I cannot say for sure. I was lying on the top bunk bed, watching everything with wary eyes. Then my father, Alberts Rošans, came in, loudly greeting everyone. His voice was booming, and something about his manner frightened me. I thought he was drunk.

Terrified, I scrambled up onto the top of the wardrobe - or maybe it was a cupboard - and refused to come down. I sat up there, removed, frightened, and watching from above. That image - of hiding from my father - is sadly the only memory I have of him.

Chapter 3
The Farmhouse Before the Storm

Apparently, my father enjoyed his drink more than most - when he could lay hands on it. Sadly, this would one day be his downfall. At the age of 76, he slipped on snow-covered steps and died.

It may have been after one such family gathering that my mother took me to live with her sister, Aunt Vera. She had married into the Bucen family - a relatively well-to-do household, with both a city home and a farmstead out toward the port city of Liepāja, in the southwest of Latvia.

But tragedy had struck them too. Aunt Vera's husband, along with his father, had been arrested and executed by the Russians in 1940. They were accused of associating with monarchists, being capitalists, one even a minister of the church - enemies of the Soviet regime. Their properties were seized by the state, though the family was allowed to remain on as "caretakers."

By early 1944, with the Soviet army once again advancing, it was decided the farmhouse might offer more safety than the capital. So Aunt Vera, her sister-in-law Marta, and Marta's elderly mother Lina, moved to the country with us children. Aunt Vera had two sons, Daumants and Vitalijs, six months and two years younger than me. They became my brothers in all but name - though they often reminded me, "She's our mum, not yours!" - referring to Aunt Vera. But she was "Mum" to me from that day forward, and remained so for the rest of her life.

I never saw my parents again before we fled Latvia.

Yet life on the farm - in the final year of war - seemed strangely happy to me. The house had a large thatched roof and a huge fireplace, where we'd hang damp work clothes overnight across stones warmed by the fire. I imagine now it was built that way on purpose - both practical and comforting.

I remember sitting on the front step, waiting for Aunt Vera to bring us the buns she had just baked, their scent warm in the crisp air - one of the most comforting memories of my childhood.

Less comforting was the large turkey that roamed the courtyard, apparently waiting for me. The toilet was in an outhouse, past a large well in the centre of the yard - which seemed to be this turkey's territory. Whenever I needed to go, it was as though he knew. He'd rush toward me, wings out, ready to peck me to death - or so I believed. I'd become trapped inside the toilet hut, terrified, until he eventually lost interest. Strangely, when I was with others, he ignored me. It was as if he had singled me out. Such were the odd adventures of rural life.

For the toilet was in a wooden hut away from the house. To reach it one had to walk past a large well in the centre of the courtyard, which seemed to be the patrol area of this turkey, which never seemed to be far away, just waiting for me to appear. For some reason it has taken a dislike to me, and I would be trapped in the said toilet till he got tired of waiting and turning his back, let me run home again. Strangely in the company of others he would just ignore me. Yes, such was life.

I also remember the farm bustling the farm was bustling with animals - geese, ducklings, hens, pigs, and a few cows and horses. Eggs were plentiful, and one day I even witnessed a threshing machine at work, though we weren't allowed too close.

There was a small stone outbuilding where sausages hung from the ceiling, alongside slabs of smoked meat - a paradise for the eyes and nose - yes life must have been quite enjoyable during the peaceful years that went before.

Back towards the homestead, in an outbuilding, there was a sauna. To venture inside I must have been quite inquisitive, for after all, I was a 'city girl'! Finding myself on a farm, there was lots to explore.

Not far away from the sauna, were some large trees with overhanging branches something that left me breathless - an eagle or hawk swooping down through the branches to snatch a duckling. I screamed, startled and afraid. Startled perhaps, the bird dropped its prize. Even now, I can see it all so clearly. I must have screamed out in fright, for he dropped it, maybe also frightened at seeing me standing there, under the tree.

But that peaceful chapter was about to close.

It was 1944, and the Soviet army was advancing again. The Nazis had invaded in 1941, after the Russians had already occupied us in 1940. That first Soviet year brought mass deportations to Siberia. Now the cycle was repeating. This time, it was the hated Soviet Security Police - the G.P.4 - who arrived with blacklists, accusations, and trains to nowhere, and periodic deportations started again.

Latvian money became worthless; Soviet rubles were forced into circulation. The cost of living skyrocketed. Resistance was impossible - our country was already overwhelmed. Communication broke down, bridges and railways were blockaded, roads patrolled. Fear and hunger were everywhere. And the Soviets resumed their campaign to replace the Baltic population with Russians. Personal wealth was confiscated;

everything became "for the public." The capitalist system was dismantled, and the Soviet lockdown began.

It may well have been Divine guidance that placed my mother - Lidija Rošans - in the railway offices of Riga at the time. She had a front-row view of witnessing what was happening. People who tried to escape the country were being intercepted and put on trains bound for Siberia. She managed to send a warning to Aunt Vera at the farm:

"Flee the country if you can."

And so we would flee - children, women, and elders - carrying only what we could, leaving behind the farm, the animals, the ghosts, and the childhood that ended there.

It was not learnt till much later on, that in the following year of 1945, mass deportations of Latvian families begun. There were to be removed to the U.S.S.R to be replaced by thousands of Russian colonists! The Soviet Government claimed that 38,000 workers had "volunteered" for reconstruction work in Russia, where they made their way on foot in the middle of winter. These so-called work gangs were actually deportations, to give added strength to the slave labour camps of Siberia. This included the building of their extensive railway line, where they died of hunger and exhaustion. Even in present time today, years later we are still hearing of bodies being found, those buried by the railway line.

However, during this 1944 year, we seemed to be living quite normally, if any life at that time could be described as normal. Maybe the Russians had not yet advanced, or settled that far away from the capital of Riga; then one day they appeared on the farm. It was during the daylight hours as I was still playing outside when I noticed some soldiers approaching. They seemed quite happy and I did not feel threatened in any way. I watched as they disappeared into the animal enclosure; and then it happened;

I can still see two or three soldiers drag a large pig and lay it on its back on a plank or board of some sort, out in the yard. Another one had a large knife. He did not use it to cut its throat - one big stab in the chest as he sliced that knife sharply down its belly! As long as I live, I will never forget the ear-piercing squeal of that animal. In shock I ran away to hide and cover my ears, in disbelief of what I had seen.

As I grow older and think back to my childhood days, some memories become even more intense. The cruelty and shock of that scene has stayed with me for ever, more so as it is almost the last memory, I took upon leaving Latvia. Strangely it might also be, the reason, not surprisingly, that I am rather fond of pigs today. Whenever at an agriculture show or such, I always try to visit their stalls, yes, even try to give them a pat!

Maybe this was the 'coup-de-grace'. I don't remember what time period elapsed or what happened next. I do remember Aunt Vera and Aunt Marta packing food and some extra clothes in a shawl or blanket; the time to flee had arrived.

Thus, early in December 1944, right at the start of winter, without ever seeing my Parents again, we left our beloved country forever, and started on our escape journey; myself, Aunt Vera and her two sons, Vera's sister-in-law Marta with her mother Lina & three adults plus three children. In the dark of night, we walked across fields of grass, jumping ditches, hiding out in a barn and hearing dogs barking in the distance.

We made it to the pier in the port city of Liepaja, with the hope of catching a ship out, unbelievably, the almighty was with us! We managed to get on board the last ship allowed to take passengers.

Full of people already, the ship was soon leaving as the Latvians sang the national anthem, 'God Bless Latvia'- (translated,) as we departed. I did not know, at being over six years of age, I was leaving my Fatherland for ever. But goodbye Latvia and hello Sweden and freedom!

Chapter 4
The Escape and the Captivity that Followed

Alas and alack! Though others had managed to flee west, this was not to be our fate. God, it seemed, had other plans for us.

We had boarded a ship named "Malgache" with the hope of freedom. But instead of sailing west toward safety, it turned south, delivering us not into the arms of sanctuary, but into the clutches of Nazi-occupied Poland. We disembarked in Gdańsk - known to us then as Danzig.

Having barely escaped the Soviet grip, we now found ourselves in a different form of danger. *From the frying pan into the fire.* Nazi boots ruled these streets, and fear changed its uniform.

Perhaps because of the trauma, I have only one clear memory of that voyage: sitting propped up in a bunk bed, inside an oversized life-jacket, unable to lie down. Maybe the bunk was too cramped, or maybe the ship was overcrowded - so many people packed together with one shared desire: escape.

We were grateful to be alive - but would we now become prisoners instead? Would this be how our story ended, after all?

As displaced persons in an enemy-held land, we wandered, uncertain and burdened. My aunts still clutched their shawls and small bundles of food. I carried a handmade little handbag with a small teddy bear inside. That teddy would later become the code used to identify me when communicating back to family in Latvia, when both the Russians and British authorities tried to reunite separated families after the war.

One memory remains vivid: we were making our way quietly through a forest, careful not to make noise. Suddenly, I had to relieve myself. Aunt Marta whispered, *"Go behind those bushes. We'll wait right here."*

Almost immediately (was that divinely guided?), we could hear men's voices approaching. Two German soldiers, rifles slung over their shoulders, were approaching along the path.

Aunt Marta always repeated how 'frozen in fear' they were - certain I would jump up and run back to them, and that we'd all be shot on the spot. *Frozen in fear?* My backside was frozen! Girl though I was, I had already learned how to keep my mouth shut long before. I sat there in the bushes, completely still.

I sat there frozen and waited. Soon the soldiers passed by us, never knowing how close they came to changing four lives forever.

Once the danger had passed, we moved on, slipping deeper into uncertainty. Our lives were not to end soon. The "Divine" plan was working. But, to have left our country willingly and to find ourselves on the run. But safety never lasted long. Eventually, we were caught. Perhaps we had asked someone for help, or perhaps we were simply in the wrong place at the wrong time. Whatever the reason, we became prisoners.

We were transported under guard by train into Germany, to the city of Rathenau, and confined to a compound on the edge of a forest.

There, we found ourselves behind barbed wire fencing - a place that, in my child's mind, looked like what today might be called a prefab. A long building, with offices at one end, a central corridor, and what must have been bedrooms or dormitories lining each side.

We were not alone, though we rarely saw the other prisoners. They stayed in their rooms or were away working during the day - as were both my Aunts, who had been assigned to forced labour.

My Grandma Lina, elderly and unwell, stayed inside most of the time. We children, however, were allowed to play in the compound yard, as long as we didn't wander.

Aunt Marta would often later laugh - perhaps bitterly - about how she didn't believe she ever put a single gun together properly. That was their assigned work: arms production in one of the factories. Forced to contribute to the war machine of the very regime that held them captive.

We were refugees - yes. But also witnesses, and survivors, in a Europe that no longer belonged to its people.

Chapter 5

Bombs, Blood, And the Bridge to Freedom

We were aware of planes flying over. Occasionally after they had already passed, we saw silver streamers, appeared floating down from the sky. We would gather them up the next day, roll them up and playfully toss them to one another. Only years later growing up I remember reading about an invention used during the war - metallic strips dropped to confuse enemy radar. Is that what we'd seen, without knowing it?

Then one evening our world nearly came to an end yet again. We were all six of us in this little room- three bunk beds against two walls. A little square table in the middle, where our food was served, only light in the room was the large domed light hanging from the ceiling above the table.

Eating our evening meal, we heard the drone of a plane coming nearer and nearer. Nothing unusual about that, we were used to the noise. But then the drone stopped.

Silence.

And then - an earth-shattering explosion. A bomb had dropped on the forest side of the building. The entire compound shook. The dome light shattered, raining glass onto our table. We froze, the meal unfinished.

There were no screams. No guards shouting. Just silence.

I must have gone to sleep afterward - maybe from shock. The next thing I remember is Aunt Marta pushing me and saying, "Stop scratching my back!" Why was I in her bed? Maybe she thought I was frightened and brought me in with her. But I don't think I was the kind of child to scare easily. Perhaps that moment planted a seed - a kind of distance that would exist between us in the years ahead.

When morning finally came, something was off. Normally, we'd hear guards walking the corridor shouting, *"Alle Menschen aufstehen!"* ("Everyone get up!"). But now, nothing.

It was I who curiously opened the door to peep out - nobody. I crept along the corridor to an alcove, where there were three or four guards, sitting or slumped at a table between then. Their heads were bent to the side, their white shirts splattered with blood.

Even as a child, I knew they were dead.

I ran back and told Aunt Vera, who came to look. She gasped, then said, "No, they're not dead - they've just been drinking wine and spilled it."

But I knew better.

After all, I had seen my little friend's dead grandmother in Latvia, lying peacefully surrounded by candles and flowers. Death had already introduced itself to me in a strangely beautiful way. And this - this was not wine.

We went back to the room Aunt Marta didn't wait long. She was already packing our few possessions, and soon we were moving quickly, quietly, past the now-empty offices. No one in sight. No sounds. Were we the only ones left alive?

Our only thought was to get away as fast as possible. We reached the main gate, and somehow - though I don't remember how - we got through. Was it already open? Had others escaped during the night?

Had we crawled under the fence? Those details are lost to time. But the fear is not. Cannot have been too traumatic, to have left no memory.

Funny how the mind picks what it remembers. I can now see us walking for what felt like forever. Eventually, we joined with other families and headed toward the River Elbe (link between American forces and Red Army). The Russians were advancing, the skies were red behind us.

Hiding out in bushes at night, endlessly walking till nightfall. A horrible memory is of a horse lying dead, beside the road, on an embankment. The horse's whole flank sliced off! I remember a potato field being dug up, anything for sustenance.

That walk lasted three days and three nights. Then finally, we reached the River Elbe with the Americans on the other side, and freedom?

But freedom isn't so easily claimed.

Hundreds of people were waiting to cross. The American soldiers were prioritizing their own withdrawal, and for good reason - the Soviets were close behind. We waited, helpless.

I watched in wonder as American military vehicles drove *straight into the river* and emerged up the far bank - specially adapted for the crossing. Their name escapes me now, but the sight remains burned into my memory.

It was Aunt Marta's persistence, her pleading and insistence that "We're Latvians! We have to get out of Germany!" that finally made the difference. An officer relented. We were allowed to cross - but there was a warning.

The bridge had been bombed in the middle, and a makeshift path had been built - two wooden planks spanning the gap, with ropes for guidance far too high for us children to reach.

We had to cross single file.

Ropes on either side were more like guide lines and too far away for us kids to access safely. For some reason, I was the one to go first. Perhaps because I had always been expected to cope, to lead, ever since my mother had sent me to live with relatives - first my grandmother, then Aunt Vera. Behind me was Grandma Lina, saying, *"Don't look down - just look where you're walking."*

Halfway across, an American soldier appeared. He came toward me, lifted me up, and carried me the rest of the way.

I was never allowed to forget it.

More than once, in later years, Grandma would retell the story - not without a note of bitterness - how I had been *carried*, while her two little boys had to walk across the bombed-out bridge alone.

Well, I suppose I was always the odd one out, and often had to cope by myself from the moment my Mum had sent me to live with my own Grandmother, and then her sister, (my Aunt Vera) out on the farm!

But now - we had made it.

We were with the Americans.

A new chapter in our lives was starting yet again. How miraculous that we had escaped a bombing? And what had happened to the other people? Granted that there were not that many, maybe they had all crept away during the night as all the guards were dead? Only now it makes me think that was why we were able to get away so easily ourselves.

We had crossed the river, and with it, we had crossed into the next chapter of our lives. We were free - or at least, *freer* - and it felt like Divine guidance had done its work again.

Chapter 6

Refugees, Relative and Rebuilding in Post-War Germany

It's interesting to note here that nearly fifty years after the war, the Americans and Russians, who had once reached the River Elbe from opposite sides held a commemorative gathering to mark that historical meeting. A moment of hope, perhaps even the symbolic end of war. But what strikes me most, in hindsight, is that even then, neither side spoke a word of the other's language! Communication relied entirely on interpreters - a reminder of how easily human beings can find themselves facing each other across a divide, with only a handful of shared words between them.

After we crossed that bombed-out bridge to freedom, the first thing I remember was coming across piles of discarded army gear. Odd-looking items, likely from soldiers or prisoners. I remember seeing square torches that could be worn around the neck, with white and green lights. I also picked up a knife, fork, and spoon joined together on a single swivel base. I had to have that. But as we walked on, we came across another pile, and realized we had to give them up again. To this day, I don't know who left them or why. Another strange, unanswered wartime memory.

We were free - but not settled. No longer prisoners, now refugees. We needed to be placed somewhere.

We were moved from place to place:

- From Tangermünde
- To Stendal
- Then to Altgarge,
- And finally to Detmold

We must have lived in Altgarge for a good many months. Aunt Marta's sister Lidija had been able to find us there through the Refugee Organisation United Nations Relief and Rehabilitation Administration (UNRA). Aunt Lidija and husband Nikolajs and their daughter, Ligita, had been able to escape out of Latvia long before us, and she had got a job at this organisation, maybe because of her extensive knowledge of languages. Aunt Lidija was well educated and well-travelled before the war years, and maybe carried some influence.

She became our rescuer. She took us from Altgarge to Detmold, where life finally started to feel - dare I say it - civilized again.

This was the Year 1946 and I was eight years old.

We lived upstairs in a spacious house, in a reasonably populated area. The downstairs rooms had been repurposed for the manufacture of women's hats - quite fashionable styles, I seem to recall. Maybe one or both of my aunts worked there - it wouldn't surprise me. We didn't seem to lack too much, at least not compared to what we had come from.

1945 Detmold, North Rhine, Germany.
I am 8 years old, on the left.

There was a calmness in Detmold - a sense that perhaps the worst was over. For the first time in years, we were no longer running, no longer hiding in forests or bombed-out buildings.

It was in Detmold that the threads of a new life began to be woven - even if we were still far from settled, far from knowing where we would eventually end up.

Chapter 7

Displaced But Not Defeated – Waiting for a Future

Not all my memories of Detmold are grim or difficult. Some, in fact, are quite sweet - moments when I could just be a little girl again, carefree, curious, and perhaps a touch too bold for my own good.

One such memory is of attending a Girl Guides evening. I was a Brownie then, and we'd gathered around a bonfire one night - the flickering flames, the singing, and the sense of belonging. I was completely captivated. So much so, that I missed the last tram home.

But I wasn't afraid.

Instead, I set off walking through the main township, weaving my way home on foot. What struck me most was the music drifting up from nightclubs tucked below street level. Each entrance seemed guarded by a tall man at the top of the steps - mysterious and thrilling to a child who had known only silence, gunfire, and fear for so long. That music, those lights - they were something new and oddly comforting.

It can't have been too far from home, but it must have been late by the time I arrived.

And oh, what a homecoming it was!

For the one and only time in my life, I received a proper spanking. Aunt Vera - my "Mum" by then in all but name - gave me a firm smacking with a bunch of tree branches. The fear in her eyes spoke louder than her hand. She had truly believed I'd been kidnapped, after everything we'd survived. That I had made it so far only to vanish - it was unthinkable. And in that moment, I understood. I had frightened the people who loved me. So yes, perhaps I deserved that lesson.

But even amid such seriousness, I still recall another light-hearted memory from that time in Detmold - a hiking trip through the forest and up a small mountain. There was some monument to see, though I don't recall much about it. What stayed with me was stopping at a tiny shop along the way, where we bought food for the journey.

I picked out a tin of herrings, neatly packed in an oval-shaped tin - and it came with a free fork. The fork had the word "rostfrei" stamped on the back - German for "rust-free." I kept that fork as a souvenir, and I still have it today. A tiny token of a time when normal life - shops, trams, bonfires, and tin forks - began to peek through the wreckage.

Shortly after, Aunt Lidija, with her talent for languages and connections, secured a tutoring position at the Baltic University in Pinneberg. When she managed to have Aunt Marta accepted as well, it was decided: we would move again.

This time, we were moving not for survival, but for opportunity.

We were still refugees - yes. Still uncertain. Still waiting.

But for the first time, the future was beginning to feel possible.

Chapter 8
Pinneberg - A New Home, A New Reality

Pinneberg, located about 18 kilometres northwest of Hamburg, had once been built to house German soldiers during the war. The remnants of that purpose were visible everywhere. At the entrance stood a large boom gate that controlled access to the compound, leading onto a wide concrete road that stretched straight ahead.

At the far end of this road stood the Union Hall, a large building where movies, concerts, and performances were held - moments of escape from our harsh realities.

It was around 1948 or 1949 that the Union Hall showed some films captured from the Germans, depicting the horrors of the Concentration Camps. This camp was now run by the British, and perhaps they wanted to educate us refugees about the atrocities committed against innocent people, especially the Jews. The film screenings were strictly for adults, yet my friend and I managed to sneak inside.

We climbed through a window at the back of the stage and hid behind some boxes near the front. The images we saw changed me forever.

One scene remains etched into my memory: a woman, weak and emaciated, holding a newborn baby, begging a Nazi soldier for milk.

The soldier took the baby from her arms and handed it to a comrade, who raised it high in the air. Then, with chilling cruelty, the soldier aimed his rifle and shot the baby dead. He shoved the lifeless child back to the mother, who collapsed, screaming and crying, as the soldiers walked away.

The horror of that moment has haunted me throughout my life, though its sharpness has dulled with time. After that, we never tried to see another film.

But not all memories of Pinneberg are so grim. Along the concrete road, I remember a strange phenomenon during a sudden rainstorm. Standing at just the right spot, I could stretch out my arms, and one arm would be soaked by the rain while the other remained dry. It happened only during certain light showers - perhaps a cloudburst - and lasted only moments. How or why this happened, I do not know. Maybe a scientist could explain it, but for us, it was a small moment of wonder - a secret amusement in a place where joy was scarce.

But I am jumping ahead of myself, as we have yet to move in.

Pinneberg Refugee Camp
(Displaced persons, notably the Baltic University in exile)

Opposite the entrance gate, just to the right, stood the first of the buildings: the university campus, dedicated to higher learning. It was here that hope was beginning to take root, and with it, a glimpse of a future beyond the refugee camp.

Next in the layout were the buildings - or as we called them, the "blocks." There were Blocks 1, 2, and 3. Block 1 was where I believe we went to school and where I attended Brownies. It was a place of learning and some semblance of normal childhood in a very strange environment.

Further into the compound was an open space - land where Blocks 4 and 5 had never been built. This empty area became a garden of sorts. I remember long rows of cucumbers, tomatoes, and even poppies growing there among other plants. It was a small oasis of life amid concrete and barbed wire.

Then came Blocks 6, 7, and 8 - and we lived in Block 6. This was our home, the place where our daily life unfolded, surrounded by all the uncertainties but also small moments of peace.

I believe it was early 1947 when we finally moved into this Refugee Camp. The buildings were two stories high, with spacious attic rooms and substantial basements beneath.

Official Refugee Document Photo.

1949 November. I am second from front row.

Pinneberg Refugee Camp.
Daumants, Ligita (daughter of Lidija), Myself and Vitalijs.

While my Aunts busied themselves organizing our living quarters, the children - as always - took to exploring. Of course, it seemed that strange things tended to happen to me more than to anyone else.

One day, we ventured down into the basement, which was surprisingly well lit thanks to large windows dug into the ground outside, letting in natural light. Almost immediately, our attention was drawn to a wooden crate standing against one wall. Oddly, every second vertical slat of the crate was missing, despite it having a solid roof.

Peering inside, as just children, we all knew and could clearly see a dead male man. What unsettled us even more was the small wooden table placed right in front of the crate, holding a glass filled with what appeared to be blood. Yet, the body itself showed no visible injuries.

Needless to say, we fled upstairs as quickly as we could to report our discovery – only to be scolded and forbidden ever to venture into the cellars again. We never saw it being removed and never got any explanation. Maybe the German Soldiers had left it behind. Obviously, some kind of ceremony? The mystery remains to this day.

Although I was not frightened at the time by what we had seen in the basement, I believe it left a subtle psychological mark on me. The hollows dug out to let light into the basement windows were quite deep and uncovered. For the next ten to twelve years, I would have a recurring dream: I was falling backward into one of those deep hollows, and above me stood a German soldier, sword raised, poised to strike my chest. I knew if that sword pierced me, I would die. With a scream, I would always wake myself - alive.

It wasn't until I met my future husband that these dreams finally stopped. Was this a sign that he was the right man for me? Perhaps it was 'Divine guidance' at work, or maybe I had been resisting the wishes of others who didn't approve of my choices. But more on that later.

Returning to the story, life was beginning to settle into a new routine - one that would last about three years.

We all six lived in the one room, divided by some cabinets and blankets. On entrance, on the left was a bench with a spiral ring cooker, water tap and sink, and some cupboards. Behind were two small beds - one for Aunt Marta, the other for Grandma Line beneath a fairly tall window.

On the opposite side of the room, Aunt Vera and us three children each had our own small bed, with another a window looking outside.

I was sent inside so Aunt Marta and Aunt Vera could have their own photo taken. But curious as always, I peeked out the window to see what was happening. To my surprise - and dismay - I ended up included in the photo by mistake. Another point scored against me in Aunt Marta's eyes for "peeping."

I am in top window.

1947 Aunt Marta and her godson Vitalijs,

The toilet facilities and communal showers were located further down the corridor. Outside every room were window-like openings in the walls - niches clearly designed to hold rifles upright. These buildings had once been soldier barracks, after all.

Despite everything, some semblance of normality began to set in. There was a commercial kitchen where we could collect food items.

I mostly remember Aunt Vera bringing back soup. We were issued milk, butter or margarine, and bread made from maize. Ration cards were used to claim these supplies, and Aunt Vera - our de facto "mum" - seemed to take charge of managing the food. She even managed to scrape together enough rations to bake a cake once. How or where she baked it, I never knew - perhaps she asked at the main kitchen?

Meanwhile, Aunt Marta had taken up tutoring French at the Baltic University, just as Aunt Lidija had before her. It was Aunt Lidija's influence that had secured our place as residents at the camp in the first place.

Overall, we didn't seem to go hungry. Occasionally, food parcels were donated from outside to the Refugee Camp. One of the oddest shipments was a load of oranges that had fallen overboard from a ship in the harbour. Since they couldn't be sold, they were sent to our camp instead. We found them quite a treat and ate them with gusto.

But the weirdest food parcels were those meant for soldiers. We discovered some small brown tins about 8 cm by 12 cm, that contained chocolate, a delicacy we hadn't seen in years. Now, this might sound unbelievable, but inside the tins the chocolate was infested with little white maggots. No sweat - we simply broke the chocolate into pieces, knocked them on the table to get the maggots out, and then nibbled on the rest. Yes, I shudder thinking about it now, but sometimes 'needs must.'

We also had small garden plots where we grew greens to supplement our diet. We'd go mushrooming and berry-picking in a nearby forest, carrying little buckets. We were always warned that if a snake was disturbed and chased us, we should drop our buckets and run. Fortunately, that never happened to me, though I once heard screams from others! Our mushrooms - mostly buttons - we'd boil briefly, then dunk in salt and eat straight away. They were quite tasty.

Aunt Vera found a job knitting for a German lady outside the camp, giving her a small income and something to occupy her time. I remember going with her several times, always proud of the work she produced. One piece still stays vividly in my mind - a cardigan in a fair-isle pattern on a green background. I must have made such a fuss over it that Aunt Vera made one for me as well.

It was during this time that Aunt Vera taught me to knit and crochet, when I was about 10 or 11 years old. Both pastimes stayed with me long after, through marriage and beyond, and I have never stopped practicing them.

1949. Also seen in the official photo of us all six, when applying for emigration overseas.

All in all, our life in the camp was quite bearable. Even clothing parcels from America were very welcome and much appreciated. I seemed to have a busy life despite everything – like going camping with the Brownies at Timmendorf, and the following year, attending a YMCA camp in August. These little escapes brought moments of joy and a taste of normal childhood. Not forgetting we had to attend school daily.

1949 Brownie Camp.
I am third from left.

1949 August. YMCA Camp. A potato peeling race. I am first in the line.

1949 May. Our Class 3, taken outside Block I.
My two cousins either side of teacher, Mrs Jekabson, myself sitting on for right. A busy year, and our last in this Refugee Camp.

Christmas was drawing near, and excitement filled the air as we prepared to put on a play along with other performances. One performance in particular was a Latvian drama, though its name escapes me now. It had two or three acts and was a cherished way for us to connect with our heritage, bringing a bit of warmth and hope amidst the uncertainty.

The cast of the Latvian play is forever etched in my memory. Below photo I am standing on the far left, dressed proudly in a national costume. Behind me, fourth from the left, is a blonde boy who had unknowingly captured my attention. His gaze, however, was fixed on the girl standing beside me, not on me.

Cast of a Latvian play.

Little did I know, this boy would steer my life in an unexpected direction. One day, as I walked down a corridor, I saw him approaching. I smiled, ready to pass by, but instead, he suddenly smashed his right shoulder into mine as he brushed past. Shocked and hurt—both physically and emotionally - I never understood why he did it. I had never shown him any interest, and he didn't look back. To this day, I wonder if it was "guidance from above," for since then, I've never looked at blonde boys the same way. That moment would resurface in my thoughts many years later, around ten years after.

So ended the year 1949, a year of both endings and new beginnings. We were preparing for immigrate to a new country, but a shadow loomed over me. There had been talks of repatriating split families back to their homelands which for me meant the terrifying prospect of being sent back to Latvia, and into the hands of the Russians.

Thankfully, a kind Catholic lady in the front office intervened quietly and destroyed my papers, protecting me from deportation. Yet this left me with a new dilemma, no proof of who I was.

Again as if by some miracle, we were led to meet a Latvian cleric, who agreed to write a statement that he had baptised me in Riga, in May 1942, and was familiar with the family. On the strength of this I was issued with a 'travel document' in my own name, and was now allowed to apply for emigration.

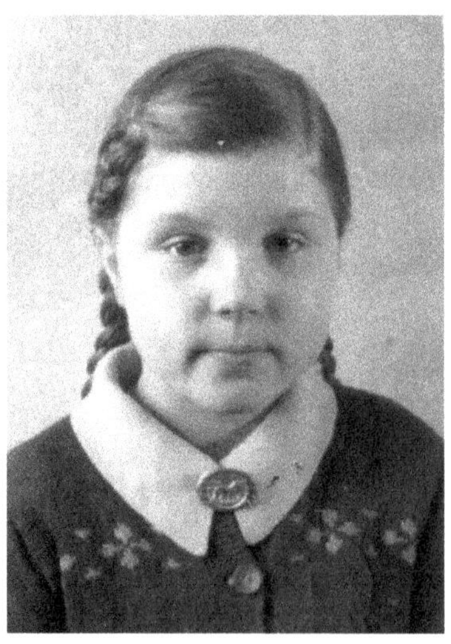

1949 Germany, I am 11 years old.

Aunt Lidija, Uncle Nick, and their daughter Ligita had already set sail for New Zealand. Although they had hoped to go to America, like many others, there was one factor that changed their course: Uncle

Nick's sister and her husband had immigrated to New Zealand after the First World War. Because of this connection, the International Refugee Organization (I.R.O.), which arranged travel and paid fares, directed them to New Zealand. We were told we would follow the same path.

In January 1950, we moved to Hanover to apply for and await our visas. There were endless appointments - doctors, dentists, and countless interrogations. Grandmother had to have some infected, yellowed, and mis-shapen nails removed. The children, including myself, attended a German school for a week, where our basic German helped a little.

Finally, the visas arrived, and we were ready to depart! We travelled by train to Paris and spent three or four days there. From our hotel window, we watched people hurrying along with long, thin loaves of bread tucked under their arms. We bought a few small souvenirs. I can remember a tiny plastic doll, only about 7 or 8 centimetres tall, with movable arms and legs. I sewed little garments for her for years afterward.

Then another train ride took us to Marseilles, where we stayed a few more days before boarding our ship. The three of us children had never seen such a large ship. Excited, we hurried down the pier to board, only to be told to pass it by and continue to the two smaller ships. Our ship was the last one, and smaller than the other. Slightly disappointed but still eager, we made our way on board.

The ship was called the *S.S. AL Sudan*. Originally a British troop-carrying ship during World War II, it had since been sold to the Sudanese government. Owned by Arabs but staffed primarily by Africans, the *AL Sudan* was now used to carry refugees like us.

Photo – 1950 S.S. Al Sudan.

Downstairs, there were large sleeping quarters filled with countless bunk beds, men and women kept in separate areas. Our group, myself and the three children, shared the same section.

It was the 22nd of January, 1950. I was eleven years and ten months old, and nearly six more years of my life had passed since we first left Latvia. Goodbye Europe, and hello New Zealand, here we come.

Was this to be a life sentence in exile? For the adults, it was almost certain they would never see Latvia again. Occupied at that time by countless Russians, Latvia would remain under Soviet rule for at least another 45 years. It wasn't until 1995 or 1996 that Latvia regained the right to govern itself, its so-called "freedom." Yet even this freedom was complicated; five decades of occupation had brought many Russians to call Latvia home, many of whom stubbornly refused to learn Latvian. The result is ongoing discord, with Latvian, Russian, and English all spoken widely.

Chapter 9
Voyage to a New Country

We must have left France in the middle of the night, for when we woke the next morning, the ship was out in the open sea. Our voyage of six weeks had begun.

With little to do, we kids were fairly free to wander safely around the ship and explore. We discovered the large dining room where our meals would be served. A spacious area filled with rows of tables and chairs, seating about ten people each. Our food was brought to us by waiters, all of African origin. I found a couple of them quite good-looking, and suddenly all thoughts of blonde boys vanished from my mind. Was this Divine guidance at work again? Only time would tell, six years later, it would indeed steer my life in a new and unbelievable direction.

Six weeks aboard a ship with no entertainment can be a long stretch. We did stop at some islands along the way. Many people suffered from seasickness. I recall one young woman who had a bunk just beneath ours, with a bucket. She was seasick almost the entire way until we reached Panama, where she was due to join her husband. Our relatively small ship was easily rocked, especially crossing the Atlantic.

Two incidents come to mind here, which may not have been the weather:

1. I was hurrying down the stairs to our living quarters when suddenly the ship jolted as if it had struck something in the ocean. The jolt propelled me forward and, unable to stop, propelled down into a run in the remaining steps, and crashed into Aunt Marta, who was sitting in a wicker chair reading and enjoying the sunlight streaming into the room. Her chair toppled backwards with me trying to avoid falling directly on her. It took others convincing Aunt Marta that the ship really had jolted to soften her anger.
2. On another occasion, just as we had nearly finished our meal, the ship suddenly tilted sharply to one side. The brown beer-like bottles in the middle of our table all toppled over, spilling their contents everywhere. Again, there was a strange jolt with no explanation.

Despite these moments, we had lighter times too. The ship stopped at the French islands of Guadeloupe and Martinique, then Panama City. Aunt Marta's knowledge of French proved very useful. Passing through the Panama Canal was fascinating, watching the locks opening and closing to adjust the water level, and the ship being pulled through by ropes attached to vehicles along-side.

Our next port of call was Tahiti, where we stayed for three whole days. Upon arrival, we couldn't help but notice a young blonde woman on the wharf who attracted a lot of attention, not only from people on the dock but also from those on our ship. Perhaps she was a woman of "ill repute," because that very night, at a dance or party attended by our African waiters, things got out of control. A skirmish or fight erupted. We only found out about it when we asked after our waiters, who had large plasters covering their cheeks and faces. Knives had been involved, and some were too injured to come to work. To make matters worse, we learned that the ship's nurse had drowned in her bath just before reaching the Panama Canal, maybe sea sickness took its toll during the Atlantic's rougher weather. This left the doctor alone to tend to all the injured.

Only now have I been forced to recall an incident I did not understand at the time. We were walking through some beautiful gardens and heading toward the bush, where we were told we could pick some kind of fruit. A Tahitian man approached Aunt Marta, who was walking with me, and they shared a laugh while talking in French. Later, Aunt Marta explained that he had offered to "buy me!" for his son, once he learned I was just a niece in the family with no mother. I was just three or four weeks shy of twelve years old! Those were different times, I suppose.

Our next stop was the island of Fiji. I vividly remember a Fijian band on shore playing music, dressed smartly in dark jackets with white wrap-arounds featuring zig-zag hems and gold trimmings. They looked very smart.

Then, for some reason, we stopped at a tiny island in the New Hebrides. It was so small we had to take boats to reach the shore. We walked along narrow tracks, marvelling at people who actually were living in caves! It was explained to Aunt Marta that it was their choice, to escape the heat. I think French was spoken there as well. It was something to see, certainly.

Finally, our sea journey came to an end as the ship passed under the Sydney Harbour Bridge and berthed in Sydney Harbour. We were taken to a hotel, where we stayed for about a week and a half. Our six-week voyage was over, and it was the end of February. We could hardly wait to get out into the sunshine.

There must have been some pocket money left, because the first thing Aunt Marta did was buy a loaf of white bread and some butter. This was a real delicacy for us and was quickly eaten outside, across the street, where we sat down beside the road.

The rest of our stay in Sydney must have been pretty mundane as we waited for air transport to our very last destination, Auckland, New Zealand.

Then came the order to get ready; we were going to fly. Now, this was real excitement! Flying! But any grand expectations quickly came back down to earth when we saw the plane, a rather small “flying boat”, resting in the water, waiting for us to board. As we took off, all we could see outside the windows was the water rushing past. The take-off felt slow and steady as the plane picked up speed and rose into the air. Must have taken a few boring hours as I have no special memory of this.

And then finally - our journey’s end, Auckland, New Zealand.

Chapter 10
A Great Plan in Motion

So started a whole new life for all six of us. Aunt Marta's sister Lidija and her husband Uncle Nick, took us to their flat at No 4, Sentinel Rd, Herne Bay. They were renting the larger of the two flats at the back of the house. This was 19th March, and I turned 12 years of age the next day.

Six years had passed since we fled Latvia, escaped the Nazis, and left the refugee camp in Pinneberg for good. I had no idea then how deeply those experiences had shaped me, or how much more change was still to come.

Strangely enough, exactly six years later, and almost to the day, my life would take another dramatic turn. The events that followed could only have happened because I was living with Aunt Lidija and Uncle Nick. I was in the right place at the right time, companion to their daughter Ligita, who was two or more years younger than me. It was a saving grace for them as much as it was for me. Unknown to any of us at the time, the "Great Plan" was already in motion!

Aunt Lidija found work for Aunt Vera in the kitchens of the Wesley Boys' Home, where she eventually rose to run the entire kitchen. A blessing came with the job, she was able to live nearby and stay close to her two sons, who were housed in the boys' home itself. That became their life for the next few years, until both Aunt Marta and Aunt Vera could afford homes of their own. Until then, Aunt Marta stayed in the flat next door to Aunt Lidija's.

My place in the family became clear from the beginning. I would often stand beside Grandma Lina, who taught me how to cook. Eventually, the cooking and the main cleaning of the house became my responsibility. I didn't mind too much, at school, we had cooking classes, so home became a place to practice and refine what I learned. By the time we moved to our own house in Kelmarna Avenue, just down the road, those routines were part of my daily rhythm.

There were lighter moments too.

We didn't have hot water for washing dishes, so I used to sneak a pot of water onto the stove after cooking turning the element on high to heat it. Cousin Ligita would keep lookout, coughing from the dining room to warn me if her mum was coming, so I could turn it off quickly. We didn't want to face her anger for "wasting electricity." But sometimes you just can't win, Aunt would come in, feel the water, and say, "Oh, this water's nice and hot, I can fill my coffee pot or teapot."

Maybe she was onto me. Maybe she let it slide because it served her too.

Aunt Lidija, highly educated, multilingual, and undeniably strong-willed—had always been the matriarch of our extended family. Each of us, at one time or another, experienced her sharp tongue. Years later, even Ligita once said to me with a wry smile, "Don't leave before I'm ready to go."

This was around the time I had some marriage offers and wondered if I'd outstayed my welcome.

Uncle Nick was hardly ever seen or heard in the house. He was a talented craftsman - painting, making silver jewellery, but his real skill was carving. He made a large, beautifully carved Bishop's Chair for an Orthodox Church in Auckland. He also carved a woman pushing a coal trolley about a foot and a half long, which was presented to a ship's captain in New Zealand. The captain's crew had once worked in a coalmine in Africa.

The last time I saw that carving was in the Auckland Museum. Uncle Nick's main job was carving gravestones and monuments at Parkinson Brothers, near the city, a back-breaking job working with granite and stone. I admired him very much. I only saw him when he came up from his workshop shed, where he spent all his spare hours carving, for meals.

So began my life with the Maulics family. Unbelievably, the cosmos needed me there, for there was no other way the chain of events that followed could have happened. But I'm ahead of myself; there were lessons I had to learn along the way, still lessons to learn from the past, as I was being gently pushed in the right direction.

Chapter 11
A New Language, A New Life (1951-1953)

At the age of 12, I started at the Bayfield Primary School. As I still spoke no English, I was put in Standard III. Not very many pupils in number, we shared the same room with Standard IV class. Though I couldn't yet communicate well, I was ahead in mathematics and very keen to learn.

Each night, I devoted myself to learning the English vocabulary we were assigned. I practiced with quiet diligence, memorising word after word. Before long, the teacher began to call on me in class, sometimes with theatrical effect.

"Zeeedra," she would shout across the room, "how do you spell such-and-such?"

She knew I would always get it right—and she used me to correct other students. I didn't mind. I had come from a place where being invisible had been safer, but now, I was beginning to find my voice.

It was here I met Enid Crocker, in Standard IV. She was to marry the New Zealand artist Graham Menary. As I had mastered enough English by the end of the year, I was promoted two classes, to Standard V. Enid and I again shared the same classroom.

Enid Crocker and I lived on opposite side streets off Jervois Road, a lovely area. There were shops up on the main road and the beach just down Wallace Road. Bayfield School was only a short stroll away. Enid even encouraged me to attend her Baptist Church for Sunday School, just two bus stops away. Our Lutheran Church only held services once a month at the Y.W.C.A. in downtown Auckland, so I was glad to accompany her.

In 1952, for memorising an entire set of verses from the Bible, I was presented with a leather-bound Bible by the Oxford University Press. To this day, it remains one of my most treasured possessions. And to this day, Enid remains my oldest friend in New Zealand.

Standard V, or Form I, came and went without much fanfare. But Standard VI, or Form II, would stand out in my memory for a rather quirky reason.

Chapter 12
Chalk Dust and Pen Friends (1953–1954)

The teacher Mr Ward, on marking my books, said he admired my drawings, especially of skeletons, birds and other biological species. He asked if I would be willing to do these for him on the blackboard before a biology lesson. When I agreed, he almost did a little dance, and we laughed, as he was quite a portly man. He also offered to fetch my little bottle of milk for me. (In those days crates of milk were delivered to primary schools for free and we had to drink them during the recess).

At the end of the year, one classmate Jeannette Gribble, begged me to give her my biology books. She intended to become a teacher and thought these would be of value to her and of no more use to me. I agreed.

It was around this time we were encouraged to acquire penfriends from around the world, using special books issued to schools. One of my main correspondents was a boy named Sadik from Ceylon (now Sri Lanka). We exchanged letters for a year or two until he became too amorous and began talking of coming to New Zealand. At that point, I had to call it quits.

I've always been interested in Indian culture. One of my best friends was Julie Routley, an Indian girl who used to attend our church. Even now, my doctor is Indian—which isn't unusual, as many are in that profession here.

Then came the big shift: high school. I attended Auckland Girls' Grammar School from 1954 to 1957. I chose academic classes, which included Latin, French, and German. Languages have always fascinated me, and I believed they would be useful if I ever travelled again. Over the years, I've added a smattering of Spanish, Russian, and even Samoan in later years.

Chapter 13
Notes, Faith and Quiet Strength

The years in high school passed quickly enough. I wasn't the sporty type, but I found my place in other ways. I joined the German Club and the Gramophone Club and was eventually made a member of the School Festival Choir.

One of the greatest honours of those years was being chosen to sing with the Auckland Choral Society in its first public performance of Bach's *St. Matthew Passion* at the Auckland Town Hall. It was an immense privilege to sing those soaring high notes in such a majestic work.

I have never been what you'd call a 'pushy' person. Yet time and again, I found myself chosen or nudged forward for things. One example remains especially vivid. During a German Club event, a visiting guest from Germany gave a special address. At the end, our teacher suddenly turned to me and asked if I would give a word of thanks, in German, as President of the German Club. I hadn't known I *was* president until that very moment!

Flustered but composed, I improvised a few sentences of thanks in German. Afterward, my teacher took a moment to praise me privately for not losing my composure. That affirmation stayed with me.

In 1956, during my Confirmation, our Lutheran Pastor, Clem Koch, presented me with a certificate inscribed with the words:

"In quietness and in confidence shall be your strength." - Isaiah 30:15

Those words became something of a guidepost for me.

Around that same time at High School, at age 14½, I began learning to play the piano. Aunt Lidija had begun teaching pronunciation of other languages to Dame Sister Mary Leo, the celebrated music instructor of girls' singing, including the now world-famous Kiri Te Kanawa. I was even sent to one or two classes to start learning singing, but soon realised it was not a path I wanted to follow.

Ligita, Aunt Lidija's daughter, was receiving free weekly piano lessons. The piano had been bought for her, and occasionally I would sit at the piano she used and pick out little ditties from memory. One day, a visitor overheard me at the piano and asked how long I had been taking lessons. Aunt Lidija had to admit that it was only Ligita who was learning.

Shortly after, I was given 15 minutes out of Ligita's one-hour lesson. Though it wasn't much, I progressed quickly. The nun who taught us began to notice. Every so often she would say, "Couldn't your mother afford to pay a little more? Fifteen minutes just isn't enough." She didn't know I wasn't being officially taught at all, I kept quiet, grateful for whatever time I had.

Our Lutheran Church, meanwhile, had taken shape. A property had been purchased on Crummer Road in Mt Eden, and we now held regular Sunday services in what had become our chapel. Soon after, Sunday school began and I was asked to play the organ for the services, along with one or two others.

I had only been playing piano for a couple of years, but the church organ was a relatively simple one, with just two pedals to keep air flowing through. I was honoured to serve in this way.

I remember one particular Sunday, during my turn at the organ, we were nearing the last verse of the closing hymn when disaster struck, one of the foot pedal straps snapped, and the pedal collapsed. With all my strength, I pushed hard on the remaining pedal to keep the air going just long enough to finish the hymn.

Of all the moments for such a thing to happen, was it just bad luck? Or another moment of divine testing? Or maybe, just maybe, Divine Intervention with a touch of humour?

Chapter 14
Crossroads of the Heart (1956-1957)

The year 1956 proved to be one of the most eventful of my teenage years.

In June, we started a Youth Club at our newly established Lutheran Church. Just a month earlier, during my Confirmation, a newcomer to the church had evidently noticed me and taken an interest. His name was Alan, and it soon became clear that he had been instrumental in getting me elected Treasurer of the Youth Club.

We gradually became good friends and began to go out on "date nights" to the cinema. Alan worked in a manufacturing jeweller's shop, and at one point, he even secured me a small job, cleaning TIMEX watches and positioning the delicate balance wheels. It was work I could do from home, and I appreciated the opportunity.

Alan spoke proudly of a large diamond ring commissioned by a Chinese customer who later declined to buy it. He hinted that it could be mine if I were to marry him, although, curiously, there had never been a formal proposal. He was five years older than me, fair-haired, not bad-looking, and, perhaps most importantly to my Aunt Lidija, very agreeable. He even offered to clean all the clocks and watches in our house, which endeared him further to her.

But something inside me remained unsettled. I couldn't explain it at the time, but I sensed that this wasn't the right path. Was it Divine guidance? A subtle warning in disguise? His blonde hair alone, oddly enough, felt like a red flag, a strange echo of a past encounter, perhaps.

As summer approached, the Youth Club organised a bus trip to the beach, and Alan brought along his small piano accordion, thinking I might enjoy it since I played the organ. He was right, I took to it immediately and didn't want to put it down.

But then, everything changed.

Just before we were due to return home, while playing in the sand, Alan dropped some sort of creepy-crawly down the back of my dress. I was terrified of spiders, and Alan refused to tell me what it was. I think it was Cousin Ligita who eventually helped by slapping my back and shaking out my dress until the creature fell out. Shaken and humiliated, I ran to the bus and sat upset for most of the ride back to the city.

Later, as we parted to catch our respective buses, Alan apologised and handed me the accordion to take home. I accepted it, gratefully, but something inside me had shifted. We never dated again.

Shortly after, I finished my School Certificate exams, and Alan continued trying to ask me back. He wanted to take me dancing. I made excuses, eventually telling him I had nothing to wear. Days later, he turned up at the house and presented my Aunt with a gift for me on finishing my exams. It was a length of beautiful polished cotton, patterned with pink and white roses, cream and grey in the background. Cunningly Alan must have thought I could make a dress and be able to go out dancing. And we never went dancing.

Then came another twist. After New Year, our Youth Club planned a picnic to Waiheke Island. I took the bus from Herne Bay to catch the ferry downtown, but missed it by mere minutes. I was devastated.

Later, I learned that Alan had brought along another girl, Norma, to the picnic. Was this an effort to make me jealous? Another test?

Again, I wondered: was this Divine intervention, one more sign I was being protected from a life that wasn't meant for me?

But before everything became clear, I still had to live through the next two months.

On finishing exams, many of us started looking for summer work. My cousin Ligita and I both secured jobs as waitresses and housemaids out at Bethells Beach, a private estate owned by the old Bethell family from England. The family still maintained cabins for rent, with guests coming to dine in the main house. The estate matriarch, Mrs. Bethell, was still alive, and she took an interest in me.

It was she who first introduced me to Tarot cards and the world of the psychic. One day, she showed me a psychic's drawing of her son, who had died in the war. Then she pulled out a photograph, and the likeness was uncanny. The sketch was, without a doubt, her son.

Then one day, the other workers, knowing my dislike of most sea foods decided to help me out. One day as I was washing the dishes, someone approached me and said they had a very tasty morsel and wanted to see if I approved of it. I had to shut my eyes, chew on it two or three times and swallow it. Trustingly I did as I was told, did not like the rubbery feel of it, but it being so small I swallowed. As I opened my eyes they started giggling and *"was it nice the piece of mussel?"*. I started to heave but could not bring it back, so drinking heaps of water had to suffice. To this day I can't eat seafood, only some plain fish. (My husband brought up in the Polynesians Islands, will eat anything that comes out of the sea, almost literally: mussels, prawns, oysters, octopus, you name it. However, he has learned that putting mussels in the microwave, he then has to eat them outside as the smell alone makes me heave).

It was while working out at Bethells Beach, that I met a boy called Phillip. Younger than I by a year or two, he was a farmer's son, and working at Bethells' looking after their farm animals, namely cows. Not bad looking and very macho and tall for his age, we became friendly, as we were separate from the people who were actually paying guests.

On a free afternoon we two took a bus into Auckland city, a movie or just fun. Having been so "rejecting" of Alan, I thought I would call into his shop to say a quick hello, and "no hard feelings? I did not expect him to come outside as I was leaving, and had to introduce him to Phillip.

Again, this was fated. Our six weeks holiday was over and I returned to school to do my H.S.C and University Entrance year, 1957.

On Sundays after Church, I used to go and visit Aunts Vera and Marta. One Sunday in early February Alan walked with me up the road after Church, and told me he wanted to speak to me. Suggested we go to the Museum Park, the Domain. A fated Sunday!

Maybe having seen me with Phillip, had it brought out jealousy in him? We went and sat down on a bench and he began by saying how much he admired me and loved me, and wanted us to have a future together. I told him I was still studying, wanted to travel and not settle down. He was getting very insistent and tried to kiss me, but I tried my best to pull away. Then he brought out a letter and said that if he posted it, that will be the end for us, as he would marry Norma and *"she's half Rarotongan"!* Was this supposed to hurt me? I tried to stand up but he grabbed my arm and pulled me down. Then I got angry and as I turned and tried to get away, he reached out to get me again. Meaningfully or not, he grabbed my little red-beaded necklace with such force, it broke and came off my neck, quite painfully.

Suddenly the pain took me back to six years before, when another blonde boy in Germany, named Arnis, had knocked into my shoulder so painfully. Was this Divine guidance, teaching me the hard way all the signs I had ignored? What are the chances, a Latvian boy and a Kiwi boy, both had names starting with 'A'?

I stood up and told Alan not to bother me again.

I also said I will return his accordion. He told me to keep it, as he had another, a larger one, and did not care what I did with it. I kept it, and I still enjoyed playing it, as I found it easier to play songs that I could not play on the piano. And it reminded me, not of him but of the strength I found in walking away.

Divine guidance had taught me the painful way, this road was not for me, and I had ignored all the signs. But God - or fate, or whatever voice guides us - had not stopped trying.

And now, the day that would change my life forever, was closer than I could have ever imagined.

Chapter 15
A Thursday Night to Remember (1957)

1957 was shaping up to be a busy year for me. I was juggling my H.S.C. and University Entrance studies, fulfilling duties as a School Prefect, taking turns playing the organ at Sunday church services, cooking at home, studying, and practicing piano.

But amidst all this, Grandma Lina's health began to deteriorate. Aunt Marta often worked late Thursday nights at the University library, and Aunt Vera was still living and working at the Wesley Boys' Home. So, it was usually up to me to babysit Grandma until Aunt Marta returned.

Then came a Thursday night in late February - a night that would change my life forever.

It was the post-war era, and many Polynesian people were migrating to New Zealand seeking work to support their families back home in Tonga, Fiji, Samoa, and other islands. Many had settled in Ponsonby, and often travelled the same routes I took to school, church, and my aunt's house in the city.

I was on my way home from Grandma's hurrying towards my bus stop, top of Ponsonby Road. As I approached the bus stop, I noticed a tall dark and yes, very good-looking young Samoan man, standing back from the stop. As I arrived, he stepped towards me and asked if I had the time?

I was flattered that he would even want to speak to me, but when I saw the watch on his left wrist, my heart skipped a beat! This was an emotion I had never experienced before.

When the bus arrived and I showed my weekly pass, he insisted, "No, I'll pay." I refused, but with the bus filling and the driver getting impatient, I relented, and said, "Okay, he'll pay."

We rode just three short stops to the end of the line. When we got off, he asked if I had far to walk home and offered to walk with me. I told him I just had a short bus ride left to Herne Bay, but he persisted, then asked if I wanted to see a movie that Saturday night, since the cinema was just across the road.

I tried to hide my excitement as I said yes, and we arranged to meet at the same corner. His name was Mu, and he was Samoan.

That night, instead of catching the next bus to Herne Bay, I walked home, heart pounding, trying to calm myself and process what had just happened. I felt a connection with him, something special, and I couldn't wait for Saturday to come.

But on Friday night, Phillip, the boy I'd met back at Bethells Beach where we had both stayed to work during the Christmas holidays, called. He had tickets to an outdoor musical out of the, Western Springs Stadium, and asked if I and Cousin Ligita wanted to join. Bonus was that Phillip could borrow his cousin's old Ford and pick us up. Nobody I knew in those days had a car, so it was an offer I couldn't refuse.

So, I wrote a note to Mu that Saturday, explaining I had a family gathering and fearing I may not see him again, asking if we could meet Monday instead. Cousin Ligita jumped out of the car as we passed the Three Lamps Road corner to hand Mu the note while I hid down in the car.

Sure enough, on Monday, Mu was waiting. We went to the movies, I don't remember which one—but after, he insisted on walking me home. I accepted gladly, even though it was about four streets to Kelmarna Avenue.

At the corner, I told him he should leave as he had to get up early for work. When he bent to kiss me goodnight, it felt natural - like old friends saying goodbye. In that moment, I knew my fate was sealed. Sealed with a kiss.

That night was not a chance happening, but divine guidance. Too many coincidences lined up perfectly:

1. Mu used to catch the bus from Three Lamps Ponsonby, to travel to his church, traveling the same route I took to mine. One Sunday, he missed his usual bus and had to wait for the next one, and that's when he noticed me on the bus. From then on, he caught the later bus, but never found the courage to speak to me since I got off before his stop.
2. Aunt Marta had to work late Thursdays at the university library.
3. Grandma Lina's health was failing, and I was the one caring for her Thursday nights, after which I walked the three streets to Ponsonby Road's bus stop.
4. Mu had music practice on Thursdays; he played clarinet in a band. On his bus home that Thursday, he couldn't believe he saw me get on, at the very same place I'd get off on Sunday mornings. That's when he planned to wait there for me.

All this happened in a span of two to three weeks in February, right after my six-week school holiday.

Coincidence? I don't think so.

Especially after the painful breakup with Alan just weeks before.

Unbelievably, over two years later, again on a Thursday night, another coincidence would happen that would strikingly change my life forever. (Pun very much intended.)

February 1957 Aged 18 years old.

Mu. Aged 22 years old.

Meanwhile Mu and I, as above exchanged photos, and continued seeing each other whenever we could, by attending a movie now and again, as we were both very busy. I especially so as it was my last year at school before University, and Mu worked long hours.

As I was taking languages, I decided to drop History and take up Typing instead, hoping this would be more useful for my future ahead. I was doing really well and passed the others in speed.

But Aunt Lidija, always the matriarch, found out. One brisk march to the Head's office later, I was firmly reinstated in History classes, as if I had no say in the matter.

So stubbornly, I played up and managed to amass 23 points in History for the whole year! The fact that I had a secret boyfriend probably did not help either.

Then one day, my English teacher, Miss Gardner, took me aside. She asked, "Is this good enough?" referring to my Endorsed School Certificate, which would help me pay for university fees and books. She also had a suggestion - why not write my life story for the school magazine? "You have had an interesting life," she said.

So, I did. I wrote pages and pages and had to shorten it all three times. I called it "Leaves from the Book of My Life," and it was the longest article in the 1957 school magazine.

And just like that, my years at Auckland girls Grammar School came to an end. University here I come!

Chapter 16
Year 1958

1958 turned out to be quite an eventful year. After years of waiting, Aunt Vera, whom I always called Mum, finally received a letter from her sister in Latvia, my real mother, Lidija. Correspondence had been banned by the Communists ever since the war, so this was a remarkable breakthrough.

Thanks to that, I was able to write to my brother, the first letter he received was on his graduation day from school!

Later that year, along with a few other countrymen and students from various nationalities, we founded the International Club at the University of Auckland. I was quite proud to be a founding member of this club, which made some waves among the other student associations.

It was some months later in the year that someone handed me a letter. They had found it on the designated area for news and such especially for the students in the campus. I was surprised, as it had an Australian stamp on it, and came from Brisbane, a city where I knew no one.

Very intrigued as I opened it, I did not expect to be opening a 'can of worms', so to speak, this letter was written to me from my father's first wife. She had immigrated to Australia with her son, before the War. Apparently, she had seen my name in some magazine, (that's all she would say) she decided to reach out. This was the first I knew of her existence.

So, I wrote and shared the news with my brother who told our mother. She was furious that I was communicating with "that woman" and instructed my brother to write and tell me she "disowned me." So be it. I had only replied once, upon learning that our half-brother had been killed. Despite that, my brother and I continued to write to each other.

My Father Alberts & Mother Lidija.

My year was busy with many activities. I joined the Gramophone Club, served as president of the German Club, and took up psychology and anthropology, both fascinating, especially anthropology, as I studied the peoples of the Pacific region, their languages, and migration patterns.

More so because I was now going out, or dating my Samoan boyfriend Mu and learning a little of his language. Laughingly I must say as he was trying to learn English at the same time!

We continued seeing each other whenever it was possible. I no longer had to baby-sit Grandma Lina who had passed away earlier that year. On Sundays I took turns playing the organ in Church. Afterwards Cousin Ligita and I would visit Aunt Marta and my "mum" Vera, who lived only a short two or three streets away.

Then one day, warning bells went off. Aunt Lidija, snooping through my things, found my diary and discovered that my boyfriend was Samoan. Even more startling to her, she found some condoms. I was still six months shy of my 21st birthday.

I got called into the back sunroom for a serious talking-to about the dangers of condoms and the harm they could supposedly cause. Honestly, to this day, I'm still not quite sure what she was trying to say.

The gist was clear enough: I was forbidden to see "this man" until I turned 21, when I'd supposedly be more adult and sensible. Six months away! I kind of agreed, after all, "the heart knows what it wants."

It was October, and my first year at university was drawing to a close. With the holidays looming, I took a nursing and caring job at the Mental Institution in Point Chevalier, West Auckland. I had a live-in position, which suited me fine.

Three special memories I look away from there:

1. An elderly woman in a wheelchair, often lucid, would ask to read my palm. She carried a clip-top handbag all day, filled with the oddest things, leftover apple cores and such. At night, we would empty it for her, though she never noticed.

I had believed in the paranormal and psychics from an early age, but was sceptical. Still, I let her read my palm, and I almost laughed when she said:

a) I would be married before another year was gone;
b) I would have three children; and
c) she saw a lot of the letters "M" in my hand. This caught my attention, my beau's name was Mu.

2. I developed a very sore throat had tonsillitis, and was admitted to the sick bay. I remember the Sister saying how penicillin wasn't working well and wanted to send me to Auckland Hospital for tonsil removal. I refused, needing to keep earning, and thankfully I soon recovered.
3. Then, I got a visitor. Mu and I had gotten into the habit of meeting on my days off, taking walks, grabbing coffee, or seeing a movie. He had rung to find out I was in the sick bay and came up one evening. The Matron on duty was so impressed by how handsome and well-dressed he was that she allowed him to visit me. No boyfriends were allowed on the grounds, especially not a Samoan boy I'd been forbidden to see.

We both felt quite smug knowing the heads peering from the windows opposite were shocked, a man in the sick bay, and an Islander at that! The news spread quickly throughout the nursing quarters.

And so ended 1958.

Chapter 17
New Family Life

Then a new chapter – literally - began with the New Year. After my three-month job, I returned to university, living at home with Aunt Lidija and Uncle "Nick."

On my 21st birthday, Mu took me out, and we ended the night at his family's home, sharing a very late, special evening before I went back.

The next morning, Aunt Lidija came in and handed me a card and a parcel that had arrived that day. She gave me the card and stood there watching as I read the Samoan words of love and greetings, signed simply "Mu." Trying not to smile, I handed it back to my Aunt. But at the sight of Mu's name and the Samoan script, she looked at me with disgust and threw the card back.

Yet, she had to see what the parcel contained, a dark, beautifully inlaid Chinese musical jewellery box that played Beethoven's *Für Elise.* My favourite tune, one I still play on the piano today. How Mu had found one, no one knows. Was that divine intervention? A sign that we had some kind of support? It only strikes me now, in hindsight. And *Für Elise* remains the only piano piece I almost play by heart.

Mu and I decided to tempt fate. He kept asking me to get engaged, but how could I, when I was still forbidden to see him openly?

Jewellery Box.

So I hatched a plan. I went to Aunt Lidija's workplace at Farmers Trading Co. and told her that Mu was going back to Samoa for a while and wanted us to get engaged - he did not want me to see anyone else.

My Aunt said she did not want to hear it. Now that I was 21 years of age, I could do as I pleased, and she was not interested!

We went out that same night and got engaged.

Then a few weeks later I found out I was "expecting". Now things got serious, we must marry now but how could I tell my Aunt? I thought we'll just go to the Registry Office, and do it quietly. Fear still ruled over me. Even her sister (my Aunt) Marta had said to me. *"One day he'll ask you to marry him, and when you say no, one dark night he will stab you in the street!"*.

Even one of my best friends, who was renting near some Tongan guys, said; 'it's alright to go out with them but you don't marry them'.

It was the 1950's and prejudice ruled. We only know of two other mixed-race couples and the one did not last long.

But my Pastor Clem Koch, knew me better than anyone. When he wrote in my Confirmation Certificate, he inscribed:

"In quietness and in confidence shall be your strength." - Isiah 30:15.

But time does not stand still, it was now or never.

We booked in at the Registry Office for the end of April. Then had some silly argument, we cancelled and booked for mid-May.

Tragically Mu's brother Ielu died chasing after a taxi where he accidently left his month's rent behind! Cancelled our ceremony again.

Now two months pregnant, I was getting desperate. What were we going to do?

Then came *that night* - the night that changed my life forever.

Divine Providence stepped in.

God never abandons you in your time of need, and I am a believer.

And yes, it happened again, on a Thursday night.

I had two late lectures at University; Mu still had band practice.

We both walked down to Queen Street to catch our bus home. His stop came first, in Ponsonby, but he always stayed on for the two or three extra stops to Herne Bay, just to see me off.

We had just gotten off the bus and started walking toward my street when I was overcome with a strange, heavy feeling. I stopped and grabbed Mu's arm. Looking back, I saw her, Aunt Lidija, rushing toward us.

Coincidence again.

Another of her Thursday night lectures at the convent?

Without saying a word, she reached us and smacked me hard across the face.

"Go home!" she shouted.Stunned, I don't even remember if I said goodnight to Mu. I turned, hurried home, and waited in my room.

Sure enough Aunt came in, she called me into the dining room. I had never seen her so angry.

"You've brought shame on this family," she said. "Thank God we never gave you our name, we once thought about adopting you."

Shame? Was it because I'd placed a notice in the newspaper that I, from Latvia, was engaged to Mu, from Samoa? No names mentioned.

Or was it simply because he was Samoan?

Did she feel slighted?

And about the name - I preferred my real surname Rošans over Maulics anyway. My parents were still alive!

Then she complained I hadn't even shown her my ring. Upon seeing it, she gloated, "Well, mine was more expensive" (also a three-diamond ring).

And with that, "Go to bed."

But instead of tears, I whispered a prayer:

Thank you, Jesus.

That was the moment I knew what I had to do.

It was the jolt I needed, like a slap in the face, quite literally, that set me on the right path.

I was now free.

Divine guidance had stepped in again.

The next morning, after Aunt and Uncle had left for work and Ligita had gone to school, I rang Mu.

A godsend - he was still home.

"I'm ready to leave for good," I stated.

All he said was, "Wait, I'm coming."

It was Friday, June 5th 1959. I wrote a short note to Aunt Lidija and Uncle Nick, thanking them for the nine years they'd kept me. I apologized for bringing "shame" on them, and added how much I loved the double candlestick Uncle had carved. I wasn't sure if I was allowed to take it, since a year earlier Aunt had placed it in my room and said, "This will be for you."

Sadly, it was never given to me.

Mu arrived shortly in a taxi, helped me load my few possessions, and we were gone.

He took me to his Aunt Marie's place (Mali), across Auckland, who welcomed me with open arms.

They say things go in threes.

We quickly made our third wedding date at the Registry Office. With my £65 in the bank, I hired a wedding dress, bought some white shoes, and gave Mu £20 left over, which was a gift to buy a bicycle, which he used to go to work for the next three years or so.

Friday June 12th, 1959.

Once again, Divine guidance stepped in.

My church Minister, Pastor Clem Koch, needed me to play the organ that coming Sunday. He had rung my Aunt's house to give me the hymns, and was told I was gone and she knew not where.

I don't know how much of my story with Mu she told him, but he must have pieced together.

As I stepped out of the taxi at the Registry Office, I was stunned, the others were already waiting, including our two witnesses... and there, standing calmly, was Pastor Koch.

Shame briefly swept over me.

He suggested we cancel and have a church wedding instead. But I explained, this was our third attempt. We were going ahead.

Then he offered gently, a small ceremony at our church afterwards to receive a Blessing. With tears in my eyes, I accepted gratefully and we proceeded there afterwards.

Surely this was guidance from above.

For Pastor Koch to need me that Sunday, to find me and without criticism but lovingly to offer us a blessing at the Church instead.

I have been a church goer all my life.

That moment is something I have never forgotten, nor ever will.

It was the final seal on our marriage.

12 June 1959 Marriage - This was indeed the first day of the rest of my life!

Unknown to us, when we returned to Aunt Mali's house to collect my things, we found the family had organised a surprised reception gathering for us.

Mu's cousin, her son, who had served as his best man, helped coordinate it. The house was alive with music: guitars playing, spontaneous singing, and even a full Samoan band that had graciously offered their services. Food flowed generously, and the dancing went on late into the night.

It was joyous, heartfelt, and completely unexpected. A warm reminder of the power of community, and how love, no matter how tested, finds its way back into belonging.

The young man who drove us to our place that night was part of the celebrations. We found out the next morning that he had no recollection of the drive home! Luckily, we avoided the traditional rousing "welcome" they had planned for us the next morning, a humorous escape to end a day so full of surprises.

Chapter 18
Interlude - Threads and Echoes

The quiet places where life speaks loudest.

They say things happen in threes, don't they?

Some stories seem small, even trivial - until something lines up and you realise they were never small at all. They're the quiet echoes. The gentle signs. The tiny threads that somehow pull us into place, without a word.

1. A Cardigan for Aunt Mali

Double Knitted Cardigan.

Some months after Mu and I married, I knitted a cardigan as a thank you to Aunt Mali. She had once admired an identical one that she had seen me wearing, simple, textured, warm, and I wanted her to have one.

Maybe a year or two later, Mu and I stopped by her place, and she happened to be heading out to a wedding. I complimented her before I realised, she was wearing the cardigan I had made. It suited her so beautifully, it stopped me in my tracks. It was a quiet, proud moment. A handmade thing, wrapped around someone who had once wrapped me in kindness.

2. Gold Coast, Australia, Years Later

All these years later, now living on the Gold Coast, I decided to knit that same cardigan again, this time for myself. The pattern had stayed with me like an old tune. But partway through, I realised the fit wasn't right. The wool wasn't Sirdar like I had used in New Zealand, and something was off.

When I showed it to Mu, he said simply:

"Give it to Tayla."

Tayla (now our grandson Tavis's wife), with two great-grand children. It made perfect sense. So I agreed.

On taking the remaining wool back to the Spotlight store, I was astounded to see the name of the girl who had served me originally. On that purchase docket, printed, the name "Tayla"! Unknowing I was knitting for our great grand-daughter, the daughter of Tayla. The sign was there, as I was able to prove to them.

Coincidence?

Perhaps. Or perhaps just another soft tug of divine timing, gently showing me the threads that still weave through my life. The same ones that wove through New Zealand, through Samoa, through a cardigan, and into the hands of the next generation.

Not loud. Not dramatic.

Just quiet echoes.

And threads that know where to go.

Chapter 19
The Family Way

But back to my story. We had been very fortunate to find a small flat just off the main road south of Auckland. It was actually the corner bedroom of a house, with a kitchenette and a combined living and dining room added on. The toilet sat on a little platform outside, not ideal, but we made do. What made the location perfect was that we could walk to the shops and doctor, and there was a bus stop almost at our door. This proved invaluable for catching buses into the city, as we had become regular churchgoers.

After our marriage, I took my new husband Mu to meet my Aunt Lidija and Uncle Nick. I don't recall exactly how long we stayed, but I remember clearly when Aunt Lidija offered us my old room to live in. "No thank you," I replied, "we have a nice little flat." Looking back, this response probably came as no surprise to her.

Seven months later, on December 28th, our beautiful daughter Anita was born. We were honoured when Aunt and Uncle came for a short visit to see the baby. As they were leaving, Aunt Lidija stopped abruptly at the door. She threw an envelope down in front of me on the sink benchtop.

"*You can keep this. I don't want it!*" she said in Latvian.

Was this meant as an insult? I certainly took it as one. Inside was the sincere goodbye letter I had written when leaving her house all those months ago. Well, each to their own.

By this time, Mu was cycling daily to his work in Otahuhu suburb while I stayed home, preparing for our first child's arrival. During these quiet months, I began what would become my lifelong hobby of crochet and knitting. On Sundays, we attended our Lutheran Church at the top of Ponsonby Road, the very place where we had first met! Unlike my family's earlier reaction, Mu was warmly welcomed in our church community. Everyone wanted to meet and get to know this kind man I had married.

One Latvian lady, Anna Ziemelis, had invited us to her home upon hearing of our engagement. She presented us with an English rose tea set, a treasure I still have today. Anna worked with my Aunt Vera in a laundry, where they had Samoan friends and colleagues. Perhaps this exposure to different cultures explained why Anna and Vera were free from the prejudices that seemed to affect others in our community.

English Rose Tea Set.

Another member of our Latvian community, Mrs. Lindenberg, invited us to her 70th birthday celebration. As we were leaving, I thanked her warmly, though I didn't know her very well. Her response was characteristically blunt: "*Well, I wanted Mu to come. He wouldn't come without you, so I had to invite you.*" She was certainly outspoken, bless her heart. Both Anna and Mrs. Lindenberg have long since passed away, as have all my aunts and uncle from that generation.

In March 1961, our son Michael was born. We were now a happy family with a daughter and a son, but as they say, all things seem to come in threes. Life was about to become considerably more complicated.

Picture our tiny flat: a double bed for Mu and myself, Anita in her cot, baby Michael in his crib, and a third child already on the way. It was clear, time to look for a house! Between cycling to his job in Otahuhu and caring for our growing family, Mu somehow managed to find us a nice house in Otahuhu, even closer to his workplace.

The financing came together in threes as well: our small savings, a generous loan from the Western Building Society, and still we found ourselves £100 short. Then something remarkable happened. Lionel Pedersen, a friend of friends from our church, someone who didn't even know us personally, offered to lend us that final £100. His kindness overwhelmed us, and we made it our priority to repay him as quickly as possible.

In May 1962, we moved into our house in Otahuhu. On September 9th of that year, our second son was born. We had planned to name him Martin, but then the strangest thing occurred to me. I remembered the old wheelchair-bound woman at the psychiatric hospital who had read my palm at the end of 1958. Her predictions had been:

1. Married within a year, and yes, seven months later, I was
2. Three children, yes, indeed
3. "A lot of the letter M", and suddenly there were too many: Mu, Michael, and now Martin?

So we named our second son David instead. I had recalled the prophecy, and remarkably, it had all come true.

Chapter 20

Coincidences or Divine Interventions

Talk about coincidences. That same year, 1962, while we were still living in our flat, I started knitting Mu a thick cardigan. Winter was approaching and he was still cycling to work every day. This cardigan was done in three-ply wool with an intricate cable pattern and a zip down the front, very thick and warm. For some reason, Mu never wore it much at all. Some fifty years later, I sent it to David in New Zealand. Was it meant for him all along? Knitted in the very year of his birth? It had always been too hot to wear here in Australia, even in winter, so it hung in our wardrobe all these years, waiting.

1962 June-July, knitted 3-ply wool cardigan

From this point on, life settled into a comfortable routine. Mu worked long hours while I stayed home caring for our three young children. At some stage during these early years, Aunt Lidija gave me her old Elna sewing machine, saying she had no use for it anymore. I had done some sewing while living at her house, so this gift opened up a whole new world for me.

Now I had another pastime, sewing. I made all my children's clothing myself, with the exception of the boys' boxer shorts, which could be bought so cheaply at the time. I created all our nightwear, my husband's pyjamas, Anita's coats, and all their jackets. The nicest compliment I ever received came one Sunday when someone told me I had "the best-dressed children in church." How very gratifying that was!

1966 Cooler weather, Otahuhu.

1967 Going to Lutheran Church.

1968 August, School day

It's only in these later years that I do more crochet work, having sold quite a number at local boot sales and gifted many others away. Alas, it's no longer profitable, as the price of crochet cotton has gone up five or six times! Now in my older years, yet another pastime has taken over, crosswords and all other puzzles. I've even won a prize or two, small sums of money. But I digress.

Life was busy, with three children, cooking, bottling fruit, making jams, from my husband's well-established garden, and still taking turns playing the organ at our Lutheran Church, Mt Eden.

This brings back one horrifying moment when the organ "died" on me. I was playing the last verse of the last hymn when it happened. It was an old two-pedal organ, and suddenly, on my downward push, one pedal broke its belt and crashed down. In shock, I had to pump air with just one pedal as I finished that final verse. The Almighty was with me again!

It was then our Church bought an electronic organ and gave me the old one, now mended, to practice my hymns at home. Our neighbours, the Roger family, used to comment on the "ghostly music" coming from our garage, as the organ was too heavy to get into the house.

During these early years, we made it tradition to visit Aunts' Vera and Marta after Church. They lived some two streets away, and we would buy some take away food to have a quick lunch with them.

It was during one of these visits that, as we were leaving, Aunt Marta said to me: "*I do like that Mu of yours*" (translated from Latvian). Was this an apology on her part? Redemption, at last! I simply smiled.

Chapter 21
Samoa (December 1969 - January 1970)

When our youngest, David, turned seven years old September 1969, I decided it was time to look for work. I soon found a position at Allied Industries, a branch of Fisher and Paykel Industries, I believe.

Working in electronics, learning the value of components and building circuit boards came so easily to me that I was quickly put in charge of another production line. However, plain supervising became boring, I loved the hands-on assembly work. So I left to join another electronics company on Dominion Road in Auckland. Again, they wanted me to supervise rather than build.

But after joining this company, we made an important family decision. We would take the children to Samoa to meet Mu's mother, Telesia. She was getting old and ailing, and this might be our last chance for the whole family to meet her. We planned our trip for December 1969 through January 1970.

Then the most extraordinary, and awful, event occurred. It could have meant the death of all of us, but God was with us again!

It happened at the end of our three-to-four-week holiday when it was time to return to Auckland. Our group consisted of about thirty people, maybe fewer, traveling with a church leader.

Our departure flight was to be a B.O.A.C. plane leaving from Pago Pago in American Samoa. To get there, we had to catch a small seaplane from Apia in Western Samoa. Because of our large group size, this would require two separate flights out of Apia.

Here's where fate intervened. The church leader decided to take his half of the group first, so he could visit a church and tour around Pago Pago until the next morning. Being part of his half, we enjoyed this unexpected one-night stopover, riding buses and browsing in a large department store.

The next morning, well-rested, we headed for the Pago Pago Airport. Boarding time came and went, but we were kept waiting for the second half of our group to arrive. We heard whispered gossip about "trouble with a plane," but nobody would give us any concrete information. Finally, we were told to board as our plane could wait no longer. Puzzled but thankful, we all climbed aboard.

When we arrived in Fiji, we disembarked to stretch our legs and perhaps hear some news, but before we could learn anything, we were hurried back onto the plane.

Arriving in New Zealand and finally reaching home, it was time for the twelve o'clock news. Before we could even turn on the radio, the phone started ringing. It was then we heard the horrendous news for the first time!

A DC-3 seaplane leaving Apia that morning for Pago Pago had CRASHED on take-off onto the reef. All aboard had been killed, including a family of five! Since we had three children, everyone feared the worst for us, hence the never-ending phone calls.

After the calls finally subsided, we could sit down, pause, and give thanks for our lives with gratitude, while feeling deep sympathy for all those precious lives lost. To think that on the whim of one man, our leader who decided to take his group first to Pago Pago, we all escaped death. Was this Divine guidance in action? It's something one can never forget.

I, along with my family, had escaped death yet again. January 1970, a date written in history, never to be forgotten!

Chapter 22
Job Opportunity

Back in New Zealand, I found new work at a pharmaceutical company called "Welcome New Zealand." The job involved filling little bottles with tablets, labelling them, and packing them away, all done on a moving assembly line. One day, I was asked to fill in for the girl who normally operated the labelling machine beside me. They told me I seemed to have a natural knack for it, so from that day forward, it became my permanent position.

The reason they gave me this role permanently? The assembly line had not been stopped once to call the engineer. You see, I noticed the machine's problem: the glue consistency needed adjusting so the labels would descend one at a time instead of sticking together. Simple, really.

All I had to do was dilute the glue once or twice throughout the day, as it tended to thicken in the air-conditioned room. This involved walking around to the back of the glue machine, adding some water, giving it a quick stir, and hey presto! Problem solved. They said I had a "knack" for it, so I became the chief labeller. It suited me fine, and the work flowed smoothly.

Even so, after two to three years with this job, I was ready to return to electronics. One supervisor from my previous company, Mr. Coen Jansen. He had been in charge of the speaker assembly line at Allied

Industries, had struck out on his own and started a new company called Delphi Industries. He manufactured speakers and electronic circuit boards, my forte! I'll never forget his words as I walked in to apply for the position: "*Oh, it's you!*"

This was said with surprise and what seemed like disappointment at seeing me. When I mentioned that I had supervised at Allied Industries where he had also worked, he thought I was the young girl whose position I had taken over - but this was after he had already left. However, not only did he hire me, but two months later, when he went on an overseas trip to Japan and Holland, he made me the flow-solder machine operator and supervisor of our small group of about ten people.

As the year drew to a close, Coen returned from overseas with fresh ideas, and we soon moved to larger premises. He now needed more workers as he added a speaker assembly line as well. More orders kept coming in, requiring additional assembly lines and more staff.

The company was expanding rapidly. Eventually, Delphi Industries joined forces with another company and became known as True Test Industries.

As the workload increased, I could no longer both supervise and run the flow-solder machine, as operating it became a full-time job in itself. However, the quality checkers and assembly line workers knew their jobs so well that I could devote my time to packing the finished products - mainly circuit boards of all shapes and sizes as they were completed.

This was a finicky job, as each item had to go into a static-free bag and be carefully packed so components wouldn't slide around and get damaged. It was somewhat time-consuming but satisfying work. Supervision of the experienced workers was a breeze, and I took pride in seeing the finished products go out the door safely and on time. As my boss, Mr. C. Jansen, wrote in my reference letter when I left: "*Like a well-oiled machine.*"

But here I must emphasize the expertise of the workers and their daily dedication to their jobs! All in all, it was a wonderful company to work for, and I completed 21 years there from the time Mr. C. Jansen first employed me.

Again, it was a godsend that, having worked many years for the same company, I had accrued substantial long service leave. In 1981, I was able to take three months off work.

My husband and I had talked about taking a trip overseas. Our children were now over nineteen years of age and able to look after themselves. Plus, I had an encounter with a psychic medium that finalized our decision!

21 years married, myself & Mu, before our overseas trip

Chapter 23
Unbelievable Continued Coincidences

Again a coincidence, but I digress - about that psychic. She was an elderly woman, one of three sisters, and she had an urgent message for me. Knowing I hadn't seen my parents for nearly forty years, she told me to go and see my mother, as she wouldn't last another year, if that long.

So it was then or never, and we booked a tour around the world. There would be exciting times, some scary, if not terrifying moments, but overall it was deeply satisfying, especially knowing how badly it all could have ended! We departed at the end of June 1981.

First stop Hawaii.

We fell in love with Hawaii - the shows, the guitars, the warm people. From the beaches to Diamond Head mountain, from the aquarium to the shopping plazas, especially Ala Moana, Hawaii became a favourite destination we would visit many times in years to come.

On to California & Mexico.

In California, Mu met up with family members, including his older brother Pona. Then came a quick flight down to Mexico City, a weird experience of flying between two layers of clouds with thunder and lightning all around us. The weather had turned quite cool, and I had to buy a little cardigan. I had studied some Spanish for this trip but couldn't remember the word for blue (*azul*) and had to settle for a red one that was available (definitely not my colour!).

Temple of Quetzalcoatl.
Pyramid of the Moon in the background.

The purpose here was to see Teotihuacan and the Pyramid of the Sun and one of the Moon (in the background in photo). We climbed the latter and looked up the "Avenue of the Dead" towards the Pyramid of the Sun. Climbing to the top we could see the charred stones down on the right, coming down. We were told there had been an explosion and fire and many deaths, hence the name avenue of the Dead Many buildings had burned down.

Some years ago, I saw a television programme, that showed an underground passage that had only just been discovered leading from the Moon pyramid right up to the Sun pyramid. Deep beneath this pyramid, there were signs that mercury had been heated and indeed an explosion had taken place. The program suggested that flying saucers had visited and were responsible! Interesting, don't you think?

On our way back to the waiting, bus I stopped to buy aquamarine jewellery from one of the many boutiques lining the side of the street. This was one of the highlights of the whole trip for me.

Back to America: Coast to Coast.

We returned to California to celebrate 4th of July, then went to Disneyland, where we managed to fit in ten rides!

Onward and upward, leaving Palm Springs, on to Las Vegas, Whisky Petes Casino - the first one in the desert of Nevada, gambled 10c and won $1!

Hoover Dam.

We made a short run to the Colorado River and the giant Hoover Dam with Lake Mead, one of the largest men made in the world.

Then south thru Arizona towards the Petrified Forest, with its fallen logs now petrified into agate, amethyst. We drove alongside the old Highway 66.

Next, on to New Mexico and Santa Fe, the oldest capital city in the United States. Following along the Santa Fe Trail, we visited the oldest church in the U.S the San Miguel.

Miracle Staircase.

Next, at the Loretto Chapel, we saw the famous “Miracle Staircase”, a spiral staircase that stands with no visible support.

On to Denver, the mile-high city, with its famous U.S. Air Force academy.

Gateway Arch.
Overlooks St Louis downtown riverfront.

We travelled through the Rocky Mountains, past Dodge City, Kansas Illinois and its gateway arch, to the west. The Muny, largest outdoor theatre we watched "Annie Get Your Gun".

In Washington D.C., we visited Arlington Cemetery, to see Robert and John Kennedy graves, Robert's marked with white cross looking on flowing water. John's with an eternal flame above the plaque. We climbed the Lincoln Memorial, and went 550 feet up the Washington Memorial looking towards the Capital of Philadelphia and its Stadium.

In Pennsylvania, we crossed the longest suspension bridge in the world, the Verrazano. Driving through Brooklyn New York, we happened to arrive during watermelon season. Streets piled high with enormous melons along the sides!

What a crazy bus journey across America - so much to see and take in, but so little time.

Final Destinations: Canada and the Ultimate Goal.

Then it was onto Kennedy airport, flying out to Ottawa to meet my cousin Vitalijs and his wife Irene. Together with Irene's mother we did one last side trip, an all-day's ride by train through Toronto, to visit the Niagara Falls. We saw the famous so-called Horseshoe Falls on Canada's side and the American Falls with its "Maid of the Mist" boats sailing into the spray of the Falls.

Niagara Falls.

The highlight possibly was walking the Rainbow Bridge and standing with one foot in Canada and one in America!

We made one more last side trip was to Milwaukee. This was to pay a visit to a Mr and Mrs Zvirbulis. This was a Latvian couple I knew from my refugee days in Germany. They were childless and had actually offered to adopt me many years ago, unknown to me at the time, but it seems God had other plans for me. Still, it was wonderful meeting up with them after all these years

Then we had to say goodbye to Mrs. Karpovs who would return to Ottawa. Mu and I continued to the airport in Montreal to catch a plane to Latvia to see my mother and brother, this was the true purpose of our entire journey!

Chapter 24
Return to Latvia (1981)

The unease that had started even before we left New Zealand now really set in. I had fled Latvia in December 1944, age six, and had not seen my parents since. I had applied for a two-week stay in Latvia, but was only allowed one week. This was 1981, and Latvia was under total Russian domination. Even so, it seemed a little unfair and, if I am to be honest about it, anxiety-causing.

So, with more than just a little trepidation on my part that we boarded the plane, this "unease" was by no means lessened when we were told we were flying into Moscow first! However, that was 'plain sailing', till we reached Latvia. Then the 'fun' started.

We landed in Riga, the capital, and proceeded to the lounge to claim our luggage. We watched as the other passengers collected theirs and walked off. We waited... waited... waited. After about 40 minutes or more had passed, I began to worry. All the other people had gone and now I was getting angry, approaching the desk to enquire, I was told to "wait there". Then our two cases were brought out and put in front of us! It was so obvious why:-

On our travels through Hawaii, Mexico, the U.S.A., and Canada, we had acquired some colourful stickers and posted them onto our solid suitcases. As I learned afterward, such stickers were hard to come by, sought after, and even valuable, as the Russians did not deal in such "frivolities"! These had been painstakingly unglued or peeled off our cases. Hence our long wait and consternation. Also, the holes on the top corners of our cases showed how they had been targeted with some hook and pulled out. However, I at least knew not to argue with anyone, but just to get safely out of there.

Then it happened again: we were so late coming out that our transport to the hotel had given up and left! We were allotted a delivery van, with a driver and his mate, to transport us free of charge. This marked the end of our journey into Latvia, but could have been, so easily, the end of our lives!

We were both sitting behind the driver and his mate when we entered a forest. On our way to the hotel along the narrow road, we caught up with a Russian army truck. Seated in the back opening were two Russian soldiers. Each had a rifle upright beside him, and a large dog sat between them. Our driver and his mate, obviously of Latvian origin (speaking both languages), started pointing at the Russians, making fun of them and laughing. Had they lost their minds? Should I say something? We were in a forest. One shot from either of those Russians and all four of us could be dead. There would be no questions asked, no witnesses. Should I say something?

Then one soldier moved his rifle from the side to the front of him, and my heart nearly stood still. I think my husband, for the first time, began to feel uneasy. Just as I thought 'this is it,' providence took over. The truck turned off the road, and we continued on to our hotel, the "Riga."

Not a very happy first time back to the country of my birth! It was all I could do to lift my legs and climb out of that van, without a word of thanks. Unfortunately for me, this somehow set the mood for my visit. Trying to brush it aside, the feeling was only magnified by other, perhaps smaller, events.

On entering the hotel, there it was again. Facing the front door, sitting in a chair, was a Russian in full uniform with a rifle at the ready by his side. However, we were obviously guests arriving to stay, and seeing our passports, he just waved us on. It was then I understood what my brother had written about, the little things one could get arrested for and how careful you had to be. This country really was under strict Russian rule, 37 years after the war!

Then I had a lighter moment. Approaching the desk to sign us in, I spoke in English. Behind us in the arrival lounge was a Black man speaking in French, trying to find someone who could understand him. One girl at the desk said to the other in Latvian, "Look at what the devil has brought in!"

As I handed over our documents, I asked if there were brochures about places to visit. I spoke in Latvian. Realizing I would have understood their derogatory remarks about the Black man, the shock on their faces was a sight to behold! All I did was wave my finger at them as I walked away. It made my day.

However, have always regretted not going over to help that man with my little knowledge of French. Always follow your instinct, I always say, shame I did not carry it out. I guess I was a little frazzled myself.

Later that day I was to meet up with my Aunt Marija. I went down stairs to await her. Through the dark tinted windows I could see a woman flowers in hand, trying to see in as she walked up and down outside. Guessing it must be her, I went past the guard watching the doors, pushed them open and went outside.

Reluctant to speak so close to other people, she took me across the road to a park where stood a statue to our famous writer, Janis

Rainis. She impressed on me the need not to speak so openly in public especially where any Russian could hear you. You can be accused of sabotage, and jailed for that. Really? Or so be it.

Afterward, saying goodbye and going back to the hotel, I saw the same guard sitting there. I pushed open the door and walked past him making no eye contact. He called out to me, but without hesitation, I just ignored him and walked on, expecting a hand on my shoulder any moment. Nothing happened, I reached the front desk and hurried on up to our room. A small victory but I had won. Never did it again though. Yes, things do come in threes, all in one day too!

On relating this to my Aunt the next day, she was just horrified. "Too dangerous never antagonise them!" She laughed, but I was left with a slight feeling of insecurity.

The following day on our way to see my mother and my brother, we stopped at bookshop window. A young boy aged four or five years old, ran up and called out to his dad to "come and see" in Latvian, as he pointed to the window. His father yanked him hard by the arm and said in Latvian "Don't speak so loud in front of strangers", not knowing I was Latvian too.

A little boy, really! And it was then I realized what the communist takeover had done to this country. To live in fear every day of your life, was unimaginable. Was that why my brother declined to have a meal with us at a certain restaurant? I never did ask him.

Then I recalled my brother writing in some letters to me earlier, walking with some mates, seeing Russian soldiers approaching, he would spit on the ground in front of them! Really? And nothing happened? (Just like the two driving us through the forest to our hotel).

Then the whole object of this trip, or at least mine, was finally to take place! My brother Alberts took us to see my mother, and his.

Regardless of the fact that she had "disowned" me some years ago, I felt the need to see her at least once, as she was now 81 years of age.

The whole visit was uneventful, as her health was failing. She seemed to be bedridden as well. She had no questions and indeed no interest in speaking to me. It was I who had to ask her questions and see if she wanted anything. Completely non-committal, our conversation, if it could be called that, soon came to an end. A few more hugs and a last kiss and we were soon bound to leave. We did not want to tire her any longer, we were soon on our way.

Myself & Brother Alberts.

Outside, my brother did say that she had a growth inside her stomach, but could not say what it was, only that she had not long left to live. So that psychic had been correct, indeed, my mother died some six months later, as she had prophesied.

Meanwhile, we had two or three days left to do a little sightseeing and exploring the city and the Baltic Sea shore. Only too soon the time came to leave, and we had to pack our bags. Contrary to our badly executed arrival our departure was almost laughable! We were escorted with our bags, to the largest limousine, I have ever seen. Sitting in the back seat our outstretched arms could hardly touch each other! Our trip to the airport was indeed to be in style and unforgettable. Was this meant to influence the way we felt about our visit?

If only I could have been able to take a photo of such a glamorous vehicle, surely only used for celebrities! However, the actual departure, or lead-up to it would still leave as both a little frazzled. This flight was to take us on to England, so not surprisingly, there were very few people leaving this country of Latvia! Citizens were still not allowed to travel, so the few people around were presumably all tourists like us.

Approaching the Customs desk, Mu handed over his passport. The man took it looked inside, and then looked at Mu. Having done this two or three times, I felt a sense of laughter welling up inside me. What was he thinking - a man painted his face to escape the country? I said to Mu *"I'm going to laugh in a minute! "Don't you dare"* he said and I believe I saw a bit of fear in his face. Maybe something was wrong with the passport? It was all I needed to pull myself together. Maybe the officer had never seen a Samoan before. One wave of the hand with the passport and he let him go.

But then came my turn. He took the passport, opened it and put it down. Then seeing my hands on the counter, he reached across and pulled my left hand towards him. My three rings-wedding engagement and eternity rings, were being inspected and played with! Suddenly fear rose up inside me. There was nobody around, just Mu and I and him. Gold! Suddenly I remembered accounts of how hungry the Russians had been on invasion commandeering anything made of gold and silver. What if he pulled my rings off! What could I do!

Fortunately, my rings were quite tight, and I just pulled my hand back sharply. Not a word said. He handed me my passport, and I hurried off. Was that to be my lasting memory of leaving Latvia? Not yet, things almost got a lot worse.

Our seats on the plane were close to the entrance door, and looking at the building side on for some reason. The condition of this tarmac was just terrible, grass sprouting up between the concrete! Taking a quick look around there were only four to five other people I could see on our plane. I grabbed my little camera and took a sly photo! Nobody would believe this!

Then a minute or two later, a Russian guard, again a rifle over his shoulder, came on the plane, and turned straight towards us. Oh my, what have I done? Had I been seen? My heart sank.

"Passports" he called in a loud voice, his hands towards us. I bent down, got my bag, and produced them. He opened one, opened the other, then without comment, just rudely dropped them in Mu's lap, and walked back further into the plane. A man sitting in the middle, was pulled up and escorted of the plane! What had he done?! What had just happened? But very soon he came back on the plane, and as the door shut, thank God! We were ready to depart. (Apparently he had been given the wrong boarding stub!)

Then as the plane began to move, there came a voice over the intercom *"There will be no taking photo graphs while in or over Soviet! Territory!"* So had I indeed been observed doing just that? How easily it could have all gone wrong! I shudder to think even now, just like when Mu took that quick photo of the Russian army television vehicle, and was not seen.

Russian army vehicle.

Yes, the Gods were with us, and perhaps a weeks' stay was all they allowed us! Or, we could endure.

I let out a deep sigh of relief. Goodbye Latvia. Soviet territory indeed. Just another sad reminder Latvia was overrun and still under the strict rule of Communists!

Strangely I recall little of the flight to London, even though it was over 40 years ago. I was just trying to relax and think of all we had endured in one week.

Arriving in London, we could not wait to get on safe ground and our hotel above the Victoria Station. We dropped our bags and went straight out on the town to make the most of it before the next leg of our trip was to start.

Exchanging a few words between us, I almost comically realized, we were still whispering, just like back in Latvia! I turned to Mu and said, *"What are we doing! We can speak freely now this is a free country and we can talk openly yes! On the street."* Almost, as if on cue, my nose started dripping! I could not believe it, was it the body's way of getting rid of stress? Happily, it did not last long, and we could carry on.

Chapter 25
Our Journey Continues

The next day we started out on the return half of our journey around the world. But first there were sights to see in England: Buckingham Palace with its changing of the guard.

Westminster Square and Abbey, Trafalgar Square with its fountain, the Tower of London (keeping the Queen's jewels, they said), Tower Bridge, St. Paul's Cathedral, Victoria Pier, and the Parliament buildings. We travelled to see the White Cliffs of Dover, enjoyed fish and chips by the waterfront and cups of coffee by the sidewalk, and marvelled at the Seaspeed Hovercraft - the world's largest, taking only 40 minutes to reach Boulogne, France- Cups of coffee by the sidewalk.

Sea speed Hovercraft.

Then a quick dash back to London. One thing I had always wanted to see, Stonehenge!

Mu at Stonehenge.

There we were allowed just to look from the outside of the circle! We also visit the Salisbury Cathedral with its great "Cedars of Lebanon". Through Wiltshire and Somerset we went to see the city of Bath, and visit the Roman baths deep underground, renovated for modern day use. These I had learned about in my Latin classes at school and were a must to see.

Too soon the time came to leave England and join our Italian Express Tour of Europe.

Chapter 26
Journey to Europe

First stop Paris. We saw the Place de la Concorde, the Moulin Rouge, la Tour Eiffel, Opera House, and the Sacred Heart church at Montmartre, We visited Lake Geneva, between France and Switzerland.

Paris Eiffel Tower.

On to the Cathedral of Milan, over the Arno River to Florence, to see the Cathedral of white, red and green marble.

We viewed the Vatican, the walled city, and St. Peter's, where Swiss guards volunteer for two years. We saw the Vittorio Emmanuele II monument, the White Stairs (built by the Romans as a thank-you for escaping the plague!), the Colosseum, the Trevi Fountain, and the Circus Maximus, where Caesar watched the great chariot races from his palace. North to Siena with its red clay hills to see the Cathedral, on the canal in Venice, and the Murano glass factory.

Driving through the Italian Alps to Longarone now rebuilt, where 1962 a part of mountain buried a village now since rebuilt. Then we left the Dolomite Mountains and were driven towards the Tyrol Mountains. Beautiful chalets through the Fern Pass into Germany. Some of the loveliest scenery ever was through the Bavarian Alps. The old Heidelberg Castle, which had never been fully restored, on to Frankfurt, to the banks of the Rhine, and Belgium.

Then on to Bonn to see the famous Koln Cathedral with its twin spires 515 feet in height. Through waterloo to Brussels to see the Basilica and the British war graves in the poppy fields.

Unbelievably, the Thomas Cook Tour was coming to an end, and it was back to Calais and then England. So much seen and experienced. Memories that stay with you forever. However, one memory I have perhaps tried to ignore was a tour down some Catacombs in Italy. To see some that were untouched and occupied by the long since departed, seemed a little out of place. To allow visitors to daily wonder through, what to some are sacred places, seemed strange to me. Having said that I am still glad to have seen them!

Chapter 27
Final Leg of Journey

So back to London it was to finish the last leg of this our unbelievable trip around the world. First stop Singapore, with its very busy building program.

Mu. A visit to the Tiger Balm gardens where Mu had the courage to charm a snake around his neck!

On to Canberra then Sydney to visit the Taronga Park Zoo, across the Bay.

A last flight in a Jumbo Jet across what they colloquially call the 'ditch', to Auckland.

In Canberra we were very happy to stay those few days, with my cousin Ligita and her son. Her mother, my Aunt Lidija, was now permanently living with her daughter, whose husband was "gone away for good". The marriage had ended. This was the last time I would see my Aunt Lidija, and my cousin as well.

Three whole months away from home always on the go. Made more enjoyable with my knowledge of German, French and a smattering of Spanish to help along the way. To have lived through all that without any serious mishap as I had dreaded, was indeed an achievement. And to have been able to do it with my husband by my side was truly a blessing. Now it was back to work settle down, and try to earn a living once more. I was fortunate to have been granted this time away and be welcomed back in my old job, for at 43 years of age I still had many years left!

It was with mixed feelings that I heard six months later, that my mother had died almost to the day as was forecast by my clairvoyant. This made me even more thankful that we had made that long expensive, and yet truly enjoyable trip of a life time. Doubtless never to be repeated. It was during this trip that we fell in love with Hawaii, which was to become our favourite holiday destination for a number of years to come.

I am one of those people who can truly say they have married their soulmate. When you no longer worry about presents, birthdays and such you know you have made it. Only thing we would celebrate would be our wedding anniversary. This had been a hard-earned and almost miraculous day.

But even here we excelled ourselves.

One week early in June 1987 we had arrived in Hawaii for a short holiday. The night still young we decided to go out to Waikiki Beach for an evening out on town. Walking down a sparkle-decorated side street, we entered a bar to have a quick drink. I sat on a high stool while Mu went to order some drinks. A man approached and asked if we were married.

Unusual but "Yes" I said, some 28 years ago! And then a bomb shell hit me: it was June! It was the 12th and it was a Friday. The exact day we had got married those 28 years ago, date and all! Had this been "Divine guidance" when I made the flight booking?

I was a Supervisor, and because of a lull in work, I had been able to get leave from my job. In the frenzy of bookings, I had missed the point but must have known it was near our anniversary "God works in mysterious ways. "Indeed."

I looked around, no other woman around, and when I saw two men kissing on the dance floor. I suddenly realized where we were, a gay bar! Is that why I was asked if we were married? Mu came with our drinks and I said "Do you know where we are?"

"Oh yes", he knew that already. He can pick them a mile away. I have nothing against them, but laughing I said "You could have told me!". We finished our drinks, no one bothered us and we quietly left. Looking back, I still have to laugh. This was a night to remember, our 28th anniversary and we were in Hawaii,

But I digress. Having completed our exciting three month, adventure filled holiday around the world, it was back to the daily grind of full-time work, enjoyable as it was. Our daughter Anita had been married two years before we left on our tour and her daughter was now going on three years of age. Our two boys, now grown up at 19 and 20+ years of age, would take a few more years to settle down, but our life was our own.

One night out in the early 80's we were in Queen Street, downtown Auckland. We were passing on the spur of the moment we decided to investigate. Before we knew it, we had signed up for some dance lessons, and enjoyed their social evenings on a Friday or Saturday night.

Mu was quite content just to attend the dance classes, but I was encouraged to take it further. So in 1986, I was entered in the grand Finals and took part in the Rock & Roll, Cha-cha and the Foxtrot.

Rock n Roll. Myself & Teacher Eric.

Tango.

Myself & Teacher Eric.

I did not win a placing, but received a small engraved trophy and a second trophy for my "showcase" of the Tango, with my teacher Eric. Being more of a shy person by nature, I was glad to receive these acknowledgements of my personal achievements.

Even more so as I quickly had to sew my own dress for the Tango, as I had a slight argument with an older lady. She was an old, established member of the Club with privileges. I was stopped from hiring a certain dress as she apparently had set her eyes on it first. So be it. I had a week to make my own gown. The compliments I received for my gown and my dance, were reward enough!

Today it still hangs back of my wardrobe as I have no one who could use it as yet. So, with the end of the grand Finals our dancing days also seemed to peter out.

This same year, November 1986, our second grand daughter Lacey was born to our younger son David and Keri, followed by a son Tavis born February 1992. Then to top it off a few years later, our son Michael with his partner Lorraine had a daughter. Leah born April 1988, and son Jamie in February 1991. This added up to five grand-children.

Then it only took fourteen years before the first great-grandchild was born, little Summer in November 2006.

The family was increasing, and as we celebrated out 62nd wedding anniversary in 2021, we already had five great-grandchildren. Yes, our bit for the population count, was well established!

2021 June, 62nd Wedding Anniversary.

Chapter 28
Another New Country

But again, I am ahead of myself. Our daughter Anita and husband Stephen had planned to migrate to Vancouver, Canada. Due to their circumstances ended up in Gold Coast Australia 1996 instead. In 1998 we both decided to visit them and, in the process, fell in love with Australia. Two years later we were on the plane ourselves and ready to settle down for good. With our son David and family also migrated, it only left Michael to follow suit some years later again. All family united at last!

We arrived in July 2000. We could not have picked a worse time, as the exchange rate between New Zealand and Australia was such that we lost one-third of all our money. Still, we were very fortunate to afford a house in suburb Stephens (now called Reedy Creek) for us and our cat Charlie. It took three more moves to find the house we now live in, Labrador, with the beach at one end of our street, doctor, dentist, post office up other end, and a shopping precinct right across the street. Perfect for our needs.

To achieve this ideal location, we had bought a house in Nerang with a lookout to the Nerang River, which we sold some five years later for double what we paid. That profit made all the difference.

Having left our working lives behind in New Zealand, we could now indulge ourselves in our newfound freedom. To be living in a country where bulk-billing doctors are free, where travel on buses at certain hours free, and the trams, even a free government dentist for emergencies, we count ourselves truly blessed.

The years passed peacefully as we settled into our Australian retirement. We discovered the local clubs, made new friends, and marvelled at how different life felt when you weren't watching every penny. Mu's carpentry skills came in handy for small projects around the house, and I enjoyed the luxury of leisurely shopping trips without constantly calculating costs.

But the coup-de-grace came in 2010, just before we were ready to move into our present house. My car of twenty years, a South Korean Daewoo, had suddenly become "kaput", in German lingo. Someone, not myself, had backed the car into a wall. The resulting water leak could never be found, despite examinations at three different garages. I desperately needed a new car.

One day in February 2010 I had been out shopping. On my way home, on the spur of the moment, I decided to stop at the Sharks AFL Football Club, as I was passing. Mu and I would go there for lunch sometimes, or a Thursday or Saturday night. I would have a go at some gaming machines while Mu would take out a KENO. I had never been there by myself, so this was a new one for me, as my husband was at home resting his leg with its broken tibia.

I entered the club, registered, and went and sat down at a machine. I only put some small money in but bet one dollar at a time. All at once I got the free games and watched as the reels kept rolling forward. Suddenly, behind me, I heard a young male voice shout - *"She's got a thousand, she's got a thousand!"*

I did not understand, but then looking up I saw 1000 needed to win the jackpot. It stood at $26,535.43 cents. I had just won it!

I sat there stunned, trying to take it in, while people around me laughed and clapped. What to do now, I could not believe it. $26,500! "Call the attendant" someone yelled out to me. He came and wrote me out a voucher to take to the counter.

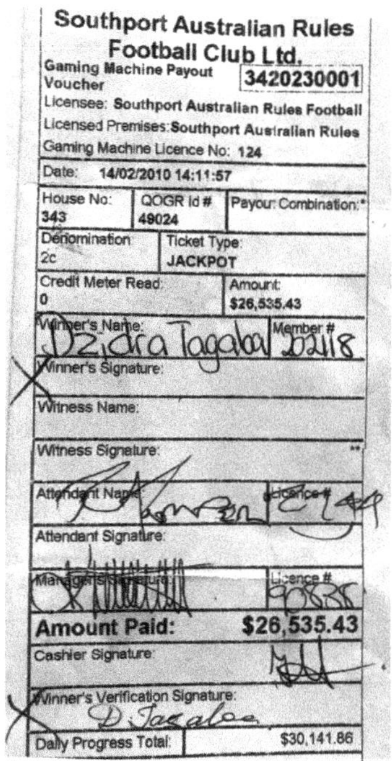

Southport Australian Rules Football Club Ltd.

Gaming Machine Payout Voucher 3420230001

Licensee: Southport Australian Rules Football

Licensed Premises: Southport Australian Rules

Gaming Machine Licence No: 124

Date: 14/02/2010 14:11:57

House No: 343 | QOGR Id # 49024 | Payout Combination: *

Denomination 2c | Ticket Type: JACKPOT

Credit Meter Read: 0 | Amount: $26,535.43

Winner's Name: | Member #

Winner's Signature:

Witness Name:

Witness Signature:

Attendant Name | Licence #

Attendant Signature:

Manager's Signature | Licence #

Amount Paid: $26,535.43

Cashier Signature:

Winner's Verification Signature:

Daily Progress Total: $30,141.86

Jackpot win!

Had this been Divine guidance? To win so much money when I truly needed it? Especially as I had an older friend Myrtle, who had befriended me and I used to take on outings to a club, casino or just to buy something, as her family lived too far away up north.

Divine Guidance or instinct. The latter being denoted as "motivation to action". Motivated by who? Or what? Have you ever said

"I knew I should have done this or that"? Was something telling you and you just ignored it?

This wasn't my first experience with what some might call supernatural intervention. I have always been a believer in such things, ever since the age of eleven back in Germany at the refugee camp. The older folks were celebrating Midsummer Eve's night, and I was outside the building with two other friends when we noticed black shadows moving on the wall. Nothing else was around - no one who could have cast those shadows. We had been told to watch if we were there. Fascinated, we just stood there until they disappeared. I never told anyone, for fear of being called foolish. Not even my nearest and dearest.

From age sixteen onward, I had meetings with psychics and mediums, and was stunned by their amazing predictions that turned out to be true. Then, to cap it all, at age sixty-five my friend Colleen told me I should be able to do "The Writing." I have been doing it ever since. Some people call it "automatic writing," but I am told it is not that at all. It's simply your guide talking to you.

I had experienced this guidance before. Like the time Mu was driving us home and stopped at what was called the "Workers Club." He said, "Wait here, I'll just buy some milk." Tired of waiting, I locked the car and went in the Club on the spur of the moment. I swiped my member's card and sat down at a pokie machine. I put some money in and pushed a few buttons. Suddenly I heard my name called out in the free Members Draw - just as I had triggered the free games on my machine.

Unbelievable! I had just walked into the club on impulse. I had to leave the pokie machine playing out the spins whilst I went to collect my $1000 from Members Draw! Mu had heard my name called, and looked in disbelief, having left me sitting in the car.

So back to my major winnings of $26,535.43. Mu could hardly believe it. On the verge of moving into our new unit, Labrador, I was able to buy a new car, my Hyundai Getz, blue at that, my favourite colour.

Yes, I have lived a truly blessed life. Mu, always the handyman, repainted the whole house.

Kitchen Ceiling.

Our youngest David, a cabinet maker, designed and installed our new kitchen. He also re-glued the whole ceiling over nine days.

Mahogany Dining Table.

Our older son Michael had shocked us by leaving school at fifteen years old, to join a cabinet making firm. At age sixteen or seventeen, he built an extendable mahogany table, which still graces our dining room today. A testament to his natural talent and determination.

Anita, through her travel club connections, treated us to a free trip to Sydney, where we met up with Michael, now being a Foreman on building construction sites.

All three children, now in their sixties, very clever enterprising!

Chapter 29
Finale

Finally, settled in our remodelled home, and having no pressing obligations, we can start living life to the full. At ages 87 and now 91 respectably, we are aware of the limited time left, even more so as the aches and pains remind you daily.

During the first 40 years of our marriage, I had been doing a lot of sewing and knitting. Indeed, I used to stay up till 1a.m. or 2a.m. just to "finish a sleeve", or finish one half of the front etc. etc.

I simply could not put my knitting down, but I have a secret! - I knit the European way which is very quick compared to the English way. In fact, while living in Auckland, years ago, I wanted to enter a knitting competition, but was barred when they heard I knit the European way.

I would love to teach this technique to other knitters. It's so simple and easy, more like doing crochet with a knitting needle - even the casting on! Once you learn it, you would never knit the English way again!

Sewing was my other pastime - all the children's clothes and our nightwear came from my hands and my faithful machine. Sadly, my old ELNA has "given up the ghost," and the new namesake is also playing up. So now I have turned to my third hobby: crochet.

Some of my Crochet.

In the last fifteen years, I had been able to sell some of my work at the local markets, but now the price of crochet cotton has gotten out of hand. So I only do it now to give to acquaintances or family, though I still have a few larger pieces I want to complete.

My other pastime is puzzles. Every morning when Mu comes home with the daily Gold Coast Bulletin newspaper after his morning stroll, I get busy with the crosswords and word games. At 87 years of age, I have become aware that sometimes a word fails me, if even for a moment. However, when doing the puzzles, I am amazed at how good my memory still is, and I surprise myself. So no time soon will I give up my puzzle craze - yes, mania one could even call it - as I have even won a few small prizes!

My husband has his own "craze" - wrestling on Fox TV. So if we plan to go out anywhere, even if it's for a meal or an evening out, it depends on his "must-see" program. But we are both adaptable, as we only have each other. Our daughter, living on the Coast as well, leads a busy life, but we still manage to get together regularly.

Sundays we watch "Songs of Praise" on television Channel 2, after which I might play some hymns on the piano. Mu seems to enjoy listening to any music, even if I play for one or two hours! He always asks, "Why did you stop?" But enough is enough, and then I might put on some CDs from my large collection instead.

Yes, life has been very good to us. After 65 years of marriage (at the time of writing), I can only thank the Lord for having brought us together in a union that "they" said would never last! However, we knew instinctively that we had each found "the one."

My two older friends I had here, have both passed away 3-4 years ago, so life has become very simple. My other way of passing time, is my piano. Was fortunate to buy the English Barnard piano at my first job, from an Englishman, whose wife had gone back to England and abandoned it. Melodies I don't have, or cannot of play on the piano, I play on my accordion, as I play that by ear.

Myself with Accordion.

Postscript

Looking back at my life it seems a dream, and not reality. Did it really happen?

1) Escape from Latvia on the last ship, and all because my mother, working in the Railway Office, had been able to warn us to flee the country because of the deportations! Coincidence?
2) To be living close to the port city of Liepaja, on the farm?
3) Hoping to go to Sweden like others before us but end up in Nazi hands in Ratenau, Germany.
4) Early May, bombed out when all the German guards were left dead and our side of the building almost intact?
5) 3-day march to the River Elbe and being allowed to cross, by the Germans.
6) All the shifting about till the English finally settled us in a Refugee Camp in Pinneberg.
7) Free trip to New Zealand by the I.R.O.
8) Then left to live with the Maulics family who organised our place there; Aunt Marta's sister and husband.

This was the "icing on my cake!" The only way I could have met my husband, through the many coincidences that took place to bring us together? Divine guidance?

At the closing of this my "epistle", the famous words of John Newton come to mind:

Through many dangers, toils and snares,
I have already come;
'Tis grace hath brought me safe thus far,
And grace will lead me home.

Amen.

www.ingramcontent.com/pod-product-compliance
Lightning Source LLC
LaVergne TN
LVHW052342100826
845147LV00021B/1149

* 9 7 8 0 6 4 6 7 4 1 0 7 9 *